SWAP
LITERACY
A COMPREHENSIBLE GUIDE

Also available from
the Bloomberg Professional Library

*An Introduction to
Option-Adjusted Spread Analysis
(Revised Edition)*
by Tom Windas

ELIZABETH UNGAR, PH.D.

SWAP
LITERACY
A COMPREHENSIBLE GUIDE

FOREWORD BY MICHAEL R. BLOOMBERG

Bloomberg Press
◆
PRINCETON

Bloomberg Press books are available for bulk purchases at special discounts for educational, business, or sales promotional use. Special editions or book excerpts can also be created to specifications. For information, please write: Special Markets Department, Bloomberg Press, 100 Business Park Drive, P.O. Box 888, Princeton, NJ 08542-0888 USA

Library of Congress Catalog Card Number 96-83204
ISBN 1-57660-001-7

Bloomberg Press books are printed on acid-free paper.

BLOOMBERG PRESS, BLOOMBERG PROFESSIONAL LIBRARY, and BLOOMBERG PERSONAL BOOKSHELF are imprints of Bloomberg L.P. THE BLOOMBERG, BLOOMBERG BUSINESS NEWS, BLOOMBERG FINANCIAL MARKETS, BLOOMBERG PRESS, BLOOMBERG PROFES-SIONAL LIBRARY, and BLOOMBERG PERSONAL BOOKSHELF are trademarks and service marks of Bloomberg L.P. All rights reserved.

This publication is designed to provide accurate and authoritative information. It is sold with the understanding that the publisher is not engaged in rendering legal, accounting, investment-planning, or other professional services. If legal advice or other expert assistance is required, the services of a competent professional person should be sought.

First edition published June 1996

1 3 5 7 9 10 8 6 4 2

Book Design by Don Morris Design

To
Myra Precourt

CONTENTS

FOREWORD

BY MICHAEL R. BLOOMBERG

THIS IS A BOOK ABOUT literacy, teaching smart people to read and interpret the basic text of the world's $14 trillion swap market. Swaps, after all, are a huge business. They affect nearly everybody in some form or fashion. Swaps allow multinationals like IBM and McDonald's Corp. to manage cash-flow transactions across global barriers.

They get new products onto markets by creating new ways for the visionaries of today—the kind of people who create laptops and laser discs—to get the funding they need for their better ideas.

Curiously, however, many financial professionals whose businesses ride on the success of swaps understand little about them. Certainly swaps can be complex. And certainly there are people who give advice on what to do. But in today's fast-moving world, what executive—indeed, what portfolio manager or financial professional—can afford to be ignorant of a market in which a single bad bet can cost a season of earnings or bring about a company's dissolution? As news headlines recount daily, swaps handled inexpertly can be hazardous to your wealth, and that of your company or fund.

While this book is about literacy, it is not intended to be encyclopedic or definitive. Our object is not to tell it all but to tell it selectively and well. To allow you, the reader, to gain a quick working knowledge of swaps, if for no other reason than to be a better judge of the advice you've received.

To that end, author Elizabeth Ungar's language is clear, powerful, and precise. In the words of swaps scholar Carl Beidleman, the book explains things "with a minimum of street talk understandable only by practitioners, or theoretical jargon comprehended primarily by academics and theoreticians." In short, the book has been written to be understood and to be used.

A Few Notes on the Format

◆ The book packs lots of information in a small package. We know you're busy. So the book is designed to be functional as well as factual, trim enough to be carried in a coat pocket and taken on the road, read easily on subway, ship, or plane.

◆ The organization of the book takes your hectic schedule into account. It can be read in bits and pieces as well as cover to cover. For instance, dip into Chapter 4: Swap ABCs and quickly learn how to record sums in company books or fathom commodity swaps. The material flows logically and offers at every turn real-world applications.

◆ Our graphics are also designed with a busy reader in mind, reflecting fundamental concepts in clear schematics and flowcharts—extending the discussion to images explaining everything from elemental back-to-back loans to diverse arbitrage forms.

AT BLOOMBERG, IT'S BEEN our goal to cut through the technical static and fuzziness of the markets and provide a clear picture. This book in its succinct content and format is an attempt to achieve that better picture, to eliminate the fuzziness. With this small book, we feel you'll be equipped to ask the right questions and to apply an informed filter to the answers you hear. It's a book that sees great virtue in being selective, from a publisher who favors short introductions.

Michael R Bloomberg

ONLY ONE AUTHOR IS NAMED on the cover of this volume, but anyone who has ever written a book knows that many, many people have a hand in creating it. *Swap Literacy* would never have seen the light without the assistance of Matt Rees, who reports on the derivatives market for Bloomberg Business News and who lent me both his resources and sources. Thanks to Matt, I connected with Robert J. Baldoni, of Emcor Risk Management Consulting; Daniel Hutchinson, of Capital Market Risk Advisors; Jean-Marc Debricon, of the European Bank for Reconstruction and Development; and Milton Bellis, of the International Swaps and Derivatives Association, all of whom patiently answered my questions and provided invaluable information. Writer Jennifer Haupt hooked me up with another key source, Elizabeth Romney, vice president at Key Capital Markets Inc., in Seattle. Just as crucial were those who read the manuscript and offered comments and corrections: Carl Beidleman, who has himself written and edited some of the classic articles and texts on swaps; Christopher Graja, senior market editor, and William Hester, market editor, of *Bloomberg Magazine* and *Bloomberg Personal;* and Tom Windas and Leslie Van Orsdel, Bloomberg applications specialists. Finally, I'd like to thank Jared Kieling of Bloomberg Press, who midwifed this baby; Ellen Cannon, senior editor of *Bloomberg Personal,* who worked 80-hour weeks to bring it to press; and William Inman, editor of *Bloomberg Magazine* and *Bloomberg Personal,* who gave me all the time and freedom I needed to write, and perhaps more encouragement than I deserved.

— ELIZABETH UNGAR

INTRODUCTION

SWAPS ARE EVERYWHERE—transforming

bank deposits, juicing up pension funds'

returns, helping to fry Big Macs. They're

the all-purpose, handy-dandy Veg-o-Matic

of the financial world. Worried your

bank's loan profits will be squeezed by a

rise in rates? Swap! Your deposits are now

fixed at a comfortable spread beneath

your lending rate. Uncertain beef prices unsettling your bottom line? Swap, and your patty cost is set.

Swaps are powerful tools that can enable you to concentrate on what you know, like making widgets, instead of worrying about something esoteric, like foreign-exchange-rate movements. No one in business can afford to ignore their use—or to use them ignorantly. Like any powerful tool, mishandled they can cause powerful trouble.

This book won't make you a swap ace. But it should make you swap literate. What does that mean? Being knowledgeable enough not necessarily to deal in swaps directly but to talk to and understand the professionals who do.

If you're not a swaps pro, why do you need to be conversant in swapspeak? Maybe you're an executive and your company uses the transactions. If you don't handle them yourself, you may still need to direct the responsible departments. And if swaps aren't part of the company's financial tool bag, you might want to know why not.

Maybe you're an investor. If you buy complex instruments, such as inverse floating-rate notes, the best way to evaluate them may be to price the swaps and simple securities that could be used to create them. What if you just put your money in a savings account, or a mutual fund, or an annuity? Chances are the bank, fund company, or insurer uses swaps to lower costs, hedge risk, or boost profits. Wouldn't you like to know why and how?

This book is intended to give you a good working knowledge of the different types of transactions, their structures and functions, their advantages and drawbacks. You'll also get a picture of the work that goes into creating, executing, maintaining, and ending swaps, and an idea of the logic behind pricing and evaluating them. Finally, you should come away with an appreciation of both the benefits and the risks involved.

The first part of the book provides a general background: Chapter 1 describes a simple swap and sets out a brief history of the market; Chapter 2 explains the basic applications, together with their advantages and drawbacks, benefits, and costs; Chapter 3 traces the life cycle of a swap. Chapter 4 consists of short discussions of topics connected with swaps and their market, in alphabetic order. (A topic covered in Chapter 4 appears in **bold face** the first time it is mentioned in one of the three introductory chapters.)

The text is written so it can be read cover to cover or dipped into. And if your interest is whetted, Appendix B and the bibliography mention some books, journals, and associations that could help you get a more advanced knowledge of the field.

1

WHAT, WHY, WHENCE & WHO?

WE'VE ALL DONE SWAPS: one Willie Mays for two Whitey Fords, my tuna fish for your peanut butter and jelly. In the financial world, the principle is the same. A simple **interest-rate swap**, for example, involves the exchange of coupon payments—one based on a fixed rate of interest, the other on a floating rate.

There are differences, of course. For one thing, the financial swap, unlike the playground variety, is not a one-shot deal. Exchanges take place at regular intervals, on the swap payment dates, over a period of time, the swap's tenor. And they are governed by a contract, the swap agreement. In this, the swappers, or counterparties, lay out what changes hands, how, when, and for how long. The agreement also spells out what happens if one of them reneges on the deal.

WHAT?

THE TERMS IN THESE agreements can be tailored to the particular needs of the counterparties. Swaps, therefore, trade over the counter rather than on exchanges, which are the province of standardized contracts. Among the simplest structures governed by one of these custom-made agreements is the plain-vanilla, or generic, interest-rate swap. As mentioned above, counterparties to one of these agree to exchange periodic coupon payments— one set determined by a fixed interest rate, the other by a floating rate, both applied to the same principal amount. All exchanges are in a single currency.

The fixed rate, or swap coupon, is generally quoted on a semiannual bond basis, as a spread over the relevant Treasury; the floating rate is usually the six-month London Interbank Offering Rate, or Libor. The principal is notional—it exists only as the basis for calculating the payments and never changes hands.

For instance, a five-year interest-rate swap might specify semiannual exchanges of six-month Libor in return for the five-year Treasury yield plus 50 basis points, on a notional principal of $5 million. If the Treasury rate is 9 percent semiannual (sa), then every six months the pay-fixed party will owe $(0.095)(\$5 \text{ million}/2)$, or $237,500; the amount owed by the receive-fixed party will vary, depending on the value of Libor.

A swap begins on its value, or effective, date and ends on the termination, or maturity, date. The time in between is divided into payment periods. At the beginning of each of these periods is the reset date; the level of the index on this date determines the floating payment that will be made at the end of the period, on the payment date. So, in the example above, if six-month Libor stands at 8 percent on a reset date, then six months later the receive-fixed party will owe (0.08)($5 million/2), or $200,000.

Payments are usually netted. In other words, although the pay-fixed counterparty owes $237,500 and the receive-fixed counterparty owes $200,000, only the difference, or $37,500, is actually paid out, to the receive-fixed party.

WHY?

WHY DO SOMETHING so convoluted? Because transforming cash flows in this manner can be a very powerful tool. Financial wizards have found myriad applications for swaps, some of which are described in the next chapter. But one that has proved most useful and durable requires little wizardry: hedging against interest-rate risk without changing a business's normal assets and liabilities.

Suppose you run a small bank. An important part of your business is loans: You lend money for 10 years to borrowers, who in return pay you interest. To get the money for these loans, you sell savings customers six-month certificates of deposit, on which you owe *them* interest.

Short-term rates, like those you pay on your CDs, are generally lower than long-term ones, like those you earn on your loans. So you have a sure profit—for the first six months. But every time one set of CDs matures, you have to issue a new set to pay investors the principal and interest due them, and rates will probably have changed in the meantime. Over the course of 10 years, it's entirely possible that the six-month rate you pay will rise above the old 10-year rate you've been receiving. And if it does, your profit turns into a loss.

You could change the nature of your business, lending at a floating rate, for instance. But that would cut your profits under most circumstances. It would be simpler just to change the nature of your cash flows. And that's exactly what a swap enables you to do.

Hedging Interest-Rate Risk

When the 10-year loans were made

Now, after 4 years of rising CD rates

Swap covering remaining 6 years of loan

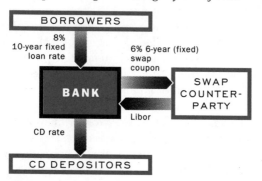

Say you hold a bunch of 10-year loans with six years left till maturity on which you are earning 8 percent. When you made these loans, the six-month CD rate was 3.5 percent. It has now risen to 5 percent, and you're afraid it may go still higher. To avoid getting squeezed further, you might arrange a six-year swap in which you make semiannual payments fixed at 6 percent (sa) in return for floating payments tied to six-month Libor. Your loan income more than pays for your fixed swap outlays. Meanwhile, your Libor receipts should more or less offset your CD interest payments. (Libor is a loan rate that financial institutions charge one another; the CD rate, which these institutions pay to depositors, is usually lower and tends to rise more slowly and decrease more quickly.) That leaves you with a profit of around 2 percent—the 8 percent from your loans minus the 6 percent you pay on the swap. It's less than your current 3 percent, but it's fairly immune to interest-rate swings.

WHENCE?

SWAPS SEEM MADE for this sort of matching of assets to liabilities. But, in fact, they were created for quite another purpose: to circumvent governmental restrictions on foreign-exchange transactions.

In the 1970s the British government tried to encourage domestic investment by imposing a tax on transactions involving the exchange of pounds sterling for other currencies to be invested overseas. This levy fell heavily on U.K. companies that needed to fund enterprises abroad. Say U.K.–based Anglo Ltd. had a branch, Saxon Ltd., in Baltimore that needed money for expansion. Because it was better known at home than across the Atlantic, Anglo could borrow more cheaply in pounds. But its savings would disappear if a tax were levied on the sterling-to-dollars conversion.

So Anglo didn't convert. Instead, it arranged a pair of back-to-back, or parallel, loans. It contacted

U.S.–based Yankee Inc. and arranged to lend the proceeds of its sterling bond issue to Yankee's Yorkshire branch, Doodle Co.; in return, Yankee agreed to lend Saxon an equivalent number of dollars.

Back-to-Back Loan

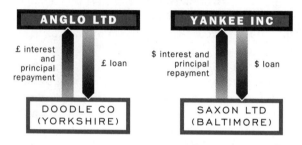

With these two loans, Anglo and Yankee both infused their branches with low-cost capital in the required currencies. The branches paid interest in the currency of their earnings, and nobody paid the government. But there was a drawback: What if Saxon overextended itself and had to default on its loan? Yankee would be out a lot of dollars. And because Doodle Co.'s loan payments to Anglo were governed by a separate agreement, they had to continue. So Yankee would also lose out in pounds.

The solution: a **currency swap**. This effects exactly the same cash exchanges—Anglo and Yankee swap equivalent dollar and pound sums at the beginning of the contract and return the same amounts at the end, making interest payments in the appropriate currencies in between. But all exchanges are arranged through a single written agreement. If one party defaults, this agreement is terminated, releasing the nondefaulting party from its obligation to make any payments still due under the contract.

Although the late '70s saw several of these transactions, the seminal swap was one arranged by

Salomon Brothers in 1981, between IBM and the World Bank. The bank issued dollar-denominated debt and swapped the proceeds for an equivalent amount of Swiss francs and deutsche marks that IBM held from bond sales in those currencies; each party then agreed to make periodic payments keyed to the other party's interest expenses, in the appropriate currencies. At maturity, the World Bank got back its dollars, and IBM its francs and marks, so both could pay off their bondholders (*see diagram on next page*).

Note that in this, as in most currency swaps, the interest payments are not netted, nor is the principal notional. Moreover, the currency rate governing the principal exchange at the beginning also governs the final exchange. These characteristics reflect a primary motivation of a company doing such a swap: to transform funds and interest obligations from a foreign currency into the one in which its usual business expenses and income are denominated, while at the same time limiting its foreign-exchange risk.

With the World Bank–IBM transaction, swaps had moved beyond their original role in avoiding currency-exchange restrictions. By linking different currency markets, they also provided opportunities for reducing borrowing costs, hedging risks, and diversifying funding sources. It didn't take long for participants to realize that similar benefits could be reaped using swaps to bridge different markets within the same currency. Thus was born the interest-rate swap, now the most common type, accounting for more than three quarters of outstanding swaps, in terms of notional principal, in the first half of 1995.

The first interest-rate swap was done in London in 1981. But once again it was a later transaction involving a U.S. institution, the Student Loan Marketing Association (Sallie Mae), that gave the market its real push.

As a quasi-governmental agency, Sallie Mae can borrow cheaply in the fixed-rate market. But its assets—

World Bank – IBM 1981
Currency Swap (Simplified)

Bond issue and initial swap principal exchange

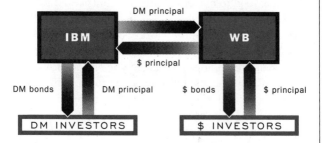

Ongoing bond and swap interest exchanges

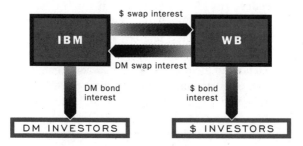

Bond redemption and swap principal reexchange

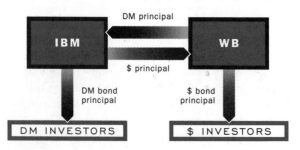

student loans—float with the 91-day Treasury bill. In 1982, the agency discovered a way to reap the benefits of its high credit without running the interest risk involved in an asset-liability mismatch. First it issued low-coupon fixed-rate debt. Then it arranged a swap: The agency paid its counterparty (ITT Corp., in the first such deal) amounts tied, like its assets, to the 91-day T-bill; in return, it received fixed payments that more than offset the coupon on its bonds. By swapping, Sallie Mae lowered its floating-rate borrowing by the difference between the swap and bond coupons.

Sallie Mae's 1982 Swap

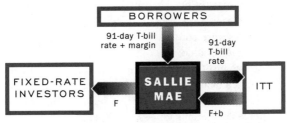

where F = a fixed rate
b = the (positive) difference between
the swap and bond coupons

WHO? SINCE THESE EARLY transactions, the swap market has expanded to include a wide variety of participants: corporations, banks, insurance companies, mutual and pension funds, municipalities, and some enterprising individuals have jumped in. It has also ballooned in terms of transaction volume, notional principal outstanding, currencies involved, and the structures and financial functions of the transactions themselves. According to the **International Swaps and Derivatives Association** (ISDA), after the first six months of 1995, the total notional principal of outstanding swaps stood at $13.923 trillion, of which $10.816 trillion was in interest-rate swaps. Currency swaps accounted for another $1.04 trillion, in U.S.,

Canadian, Hong Kong, New Zealand, and Australian dollars; Belgian, French, and Swiss francs; pounds sterling, deutsche marks, lire, yen, and ECUs, as well as smaller amounts in other currencies.

In addition to currency and interest-rate swaps, there are now **commodity swaps**, **equity swaps**, even **art-market swaps**. Moreover, almost every element of the plain-vanilla structure—from the timing of rate setting and ending and commencement dates, to the type and speed of cash flows, to the treatment of principal—has been modified to form so-called **nongeneric swaps**: **forward**, **zero-coupon**, and **amortizing**, among other varieties. Options on swaps, or **swaptions**, also exist.

As the market has become larger and more complex, the way swaps are conducted has changed. The first swaps were counterparty transactions. A middleman—usually a commercial or investment bank—found two institutions with complementary needs and brokered a deal between them, negotiating with each on behalf of the other. For this service, the broker earned a flat commission—say, 0.5 percent of the principal—and the two parties made their periodic payments directly to one another.

Swap Broker

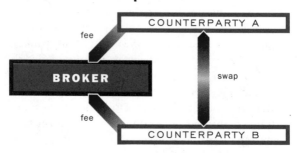

This arrangement quickly became inefficient. Increasing swap volume reduced the intermarket discrepancies that the transactions exploited, so deals had to be concluded fast to capture fleeting opportunities. Users' specialized needs, however, made it difficult for brokers to find matches quickly. As a result, many took the opposite sides themselves, becoming swap dealers, or market makers.

Taking the opposite side of a client's swap expedites the transaction. But it also entails taking a position, say on the direction of interest rates. If the dealer does not want this exposure, it will seek an offsetting swap with another counterparty or, if a perfect match can't be found, several swaps with multiple counterparties that together cover its liability. For the life of the swap, the dealer stands in the middle, passing payments from one end user to another and earning a steady profit stream from the bid-ask spread: Complementary deals are generally structured so that floating payments off-set each other, but the fixed rate the dealer receives (the ask) is greater than the one it pays (the bid). The difference between the two fixed rates is the dealer's spread, arrived at by choosing a midrate, then adding a certain number of basis points to get the ask and sub-tracting the same number for the bid.

Swap Dealer

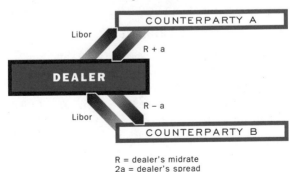

R = dealer's midrate
2a = dealer's spread

The spread is the price dealers exact not only for providing the customized cash flows customers need, when they need them, but also for taking on **risks**. Among these are **credit** and **default risk**: the likelihood that a particular counterparty will fail to honor an obligation and the extent of the financial injury the dealer would sustain if it did.

In the older, brokering arrangement, these risks were borne by the counterparties themselves. A broker removes itself from the swap once the agreement is finalized. But a dealer, usually a highly rated bank or other financial institution, remains in the middle and must honor a swap agreement with one party even if its counterparty in the offsetting transaction defaults. It thus takes on credit risk from all sides of every swap deal it arranges.

Another risk the intermediary runs is that interest rates will move against it before counterparties to offsetting swaps can be found, or that these swaps won't be perfect matches to the original one and so leave it partially exposed. A dealer may hedge against this risk by taking the appropriate long or short position in a standard debt instrument. U.S. Treasuries, with their liquid market and broad range of maturities, have been favorite hedges. Hence the fact that a swap's fixed rate is often quoted as a spread over the Treasury security with the closest maturity.

Conclusion

NOW YOU KNOW how a simple swap works and how its structure and market have evolved. So far, though, you've seen it at work only in asset-liability mismatches and cross-currency bond deals. In the course of their evolution, swaps have developed a range of applications. The next chapter will introduce you to them.

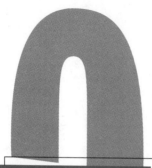

HOW, WHEN & WHETHER TO USE SWAPS

HOW COULD YOU USE SWAPS? That depends on your business. Combined with a variety of instruments, including other swaps, these transactions perform many roles. Attached to debt securities (**liability** or **liability-based swaps**), they can lower present and future borrowing costs and prevent losses from shifts in interest and currency-exchange rates; in combination with income-producing investments (**asset** or **asset-based swaps**), they may boost or stabilize returns and protect profits against adverse price, interest, or currency movements. That's just a sampling.

Swaps are very flexible tools, with many

applications you might find tempting. But, like any instrument, they have costs as well as benefits that have to be factored into your financial strategy decisions. This chapter will sketch in both sides of the equation.

Swap applications are often grouped into three broad categories: arbitrage, hedging, and speculation. This classification doesn't exhaust all the possibilities, but it does provide a useful framework for an introductory discussion. In Chapter 4, the entries for the different types of swaps include descriptions of some of the functions specific to each structure.

Arbitrage: Squeezing Out an Advantage

AN ARBITRAGEUR EXPLOITS THE differences between the costs of similar items in different markets to make a risk-free profit. Because swaps link markets—providing a conduit for exchanging, say, fixed for floating rates or Swiss funds for German—they are ideal tools for arbitraging borrowing costs down or asset profits up. Consider an example of what is sometimes called new-issue arbitrage.

Midwest regional supermarket chain R&B wants to expand into the Southwest. To do this, it needs $1 million in new funds. But the company has a B credit rating, which makes a public fixed-rate debt offering expensive: five-year bonds for R&B's credit and industry sector are yielding 10.5 percent sa, 200 basis points over Treasuries with the same maturity and 150bp above the 9 percent yield for AA-rated bonds. As R&B's treasurer, you know the yield spread between B and AA credits is narrower in the market for floating-rate notes—75bp over Libor (B) versus 25bp under (AA), for a 100bp difference. But your CEO wants to make sure that the debt element of the company's expenses is fixed and predictable. What do you do?

You could use a swap to arbitrage the difference between credit-risk spreads in the two markets into lower fixed funding costs for your company. All you need is a AA-rated company willing to consider floating-rate debt. You find one in Classic Corp., a chemicals manufacturer whose treasurer foresees a drop in interest rates and would like to see the company's funding costs drop with them.

Each corporation now goes to the market that offers it the most favorable credit-risk spread—R&B issues $1 million of five-year FRNs yielding Libor plus 75; Classic, five-year bonds with a fixed 9 percent sa coupon. Next, they swap: R&B agrees to pay Classic 9.5 percent sa on a notional principal of $1 million every six months for five years in return for receiving six-month Libor.

New-Issue Arbitrage

Bond issue

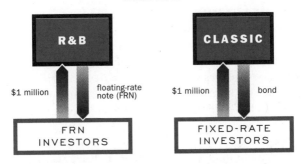

Swap and bond interest payments

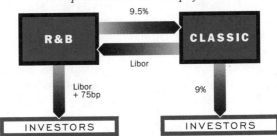

The result: R&B gets fixed-rate debt at approximately 10.25 percent sa; Classic, a floating-rate obligation of Libor minus about 50bp. Both save around 25bp by not going directly to the market for their preferred type of funding. (Figures are approximate because they don't take into account different day-count conventions.)

Income (+) and Outflow (–)

	R&B	Classic
FRN:	– (Libor + .75%)	
Bond:		–9.0%
Swap:	+ Libor	– Libor
	–9.5%	+9.5%
Total:	–10.25%	– (Libor – 50bp)
Market issue:	–10.50%	– (Libor – 25bp)

COMPARATIVE ADVANTAGE R&B's swap with Classic was possible because the yield spread between B- and AA-rated credits was greater in the fixed- than in the floating-rate market. By splitting the difference, both companies were able to lower their borrowing costs. Of course, in the real world, the split would not be 50-50. The higher credit, negotiating from the position of power, would probably get the lion's share of the savings. And both margins might be shaved by the interposition of a swap dealer. The dealer, acting as middleman, would find the counterparties, arrange the deal, mediate the cash flows, take on the credit risk—and compensate itself with a bid-ask spread. For instance, it might arrange to receive 9.6 percent from R&B and pay out only 9.45 percent to Classic. The dealer would pocket 15bp per payment, while R&B's and Classic's funding costs would rise to 10.35 percent and Libor – 45bp, respectively.

The important point here, however, is that two different markets assigned different values to the same

Mediated Arbitrage

credit gap. In describing situations like this, the term "comparative advantage" is often used (a reference to the principle formulated by David Ricardo in the 19th century to explain international trade). Clearly, Classic has an *absolute* advantage over R&B in both the fixed- and floating-rate markets. But its advantage is smaller in the latter. So R&B is said to have a comparative, or relative, advantage in the floating market, while Classic has a comparative, as well as an absolute, advantage in the fixed market.

Whenever potential counterparties have comparative advantages in different markets, arbitrage is possible. The pricing disparities exploited have several sources. The different credit-risk spreads for fixed and floating issues, for example, are sometimes attributed to the different sets of investors the two markets attract: Institutions and retail investors, who are the main fixed-rate debt buyers, are less experienced in evaluating credit risks than banks, the primary buyers of floating-rate notes, and so require larger spreads to protect them against default.

Finance also has a version of home-field advantage.

A corporation that needs foreign funds may find it cheaper to borrow in its domestic market and swap than to go directly to the foreign market, where it is less well known or where the government imposes restrictive taxes on income from nondomestic investments. That was the situation in which British Anglo Ltd. and American Yankee Corp. found themselves in Chapter 1: both needed to send money to branches abroad but could issue debt at lower rates at home. In the example, the two companies solved their problem with a parallel loan, but a currency swap would have accomplished the same thing: Anglo and Yankee would borrow equivalent amounts of pounds and dollars, respectively; they would then exchange these funds and make each other's bond-interest payments throughout the swap tenor, finally reexchanging the principal at the end.

On the other hand, a borrower is sometimes too well known in a market—it has issued so often or in such great volume that investors are unwilling to buy more of its bonds for their portfolios unless they get a higher yield. Conversely, high-credit-quality issuers often command premium prices in markets where they are underrepresented and portfolio managers are eager for diversification. These types of situations formed the background for the World Bank–IBM deal, also discussed in Chapter 1. The bank's huge borrowing requirements had led to saturation of the markets it favored—those where interest rates were low, like the German and Swiss. These same markets looked favorably on the debt of IBM, which had excellent credit but little presence there. So the World Bank had a comparative advantage in dollars and the American company in marks and francs.

Assets can be arbitraged as well as liabilities, to increase a portfolio's returns. For instance, after the RJR/Nabisco megamerger in the late 1980s, cautious investors shied away from corporate bonds in general, causing new issues to dry up and spreads over Treasuries to widen in the secondary market. An FRN investor, such as a bank, with a contrarian view could have bought high-quality corporates cheaply, then entered into a pay-fixed interest-rate swap. The inflated rate it received on the corporate bonds would more than cancel out the fixed rate it paid on the swap, so the bank would wind up with a synthetic floating asset yielding a sizable spread over Libor.

Asset Arbitrage

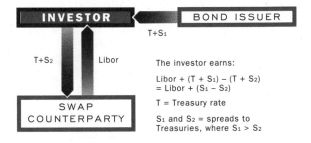

INVESTOR ◄──── BOND ISSUER

$T + S_1$

$T + S_2$ Libor

SWAP
COUNTERPARTY

The investor earns:

$Libor + (T + S_1) - (T + S_2)$
$= Libor + (S_1 - S_2)$

T = Treasury rate

S_1 and S_2 = spreads to
Treasuries, where $S_1 > S_2$

Hedging:
Two Risks Make a Right

ARBITRAGE IS USED to lower costs or boost profits; hedging is used to prevent losses. The process involves offsetting the risk inherent in an existing position by taking another position that entails the opposite risk. For example, the small bank described in Chapter 1 had fixed-rate income, from loans, and variable-rate liabilities, in the form of deposits. The mismatch exposed it to interest-rate risk: rising short-term rates would reduce, or even reverse, its profits. The bank managed this exposure by entering into a pay-fixed swap, which has the opposite risk profile: in the same situation—rising rates—where the loan-and-deposit business nets less money, the swap earns more.

Swaps are also used to hedge commodity-price risk.

Say you're the treasurer of ¡Yo, Soy!, which operates a chain of Tex-Mex tofu-burger joints. One of your major expense items is soybeans, whose price goes up and down. Because of heavy competition, you can't afford to change what you charge for burgers to compensate, so your profits also go up and down.

To even out your net income, you could do a commodity swap: You arrange to pay a counterparty, every quarter for five years, a fixed price on a notional delivery of soybeans, the size of the delivery determined by your expected soy consumption. In return, your counterparty pays you a variable price, based on the soy spot rate, applied to the same notional quantity. The spot payments the company receives from the swap offset those it makes in the market for the actual commodity. So its soybean expense is locked in at the fixed price it pays under the swap, and a profit margin is assured.

Price Hedge

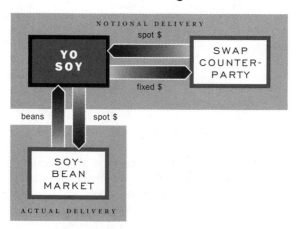

Speculation: What If?

HEDGING SPARES YOU unpleasant surprises when prices or rates move against you. But it also prevents you from profiting when the movements are in your favor: The bank gets a predictable, modest profit from the difference between its loan rate and swap coupon, but it gives up potential windfalls if the gap between its loan and deposit rates widens. ¡Yo, Soy! locks in its ingredient cost, but it loses the opportunity to gain from a drop in the bean price.

Swaps can also be used for the opposite purpose—to enhance the profit potential of your portfolio or balance sheet by making it more sensitive to economic changes. Of course, doing this exposes you to much greater losses as well.

Say you're the CFO of a mortgage company that raises the money it lends out by issuing fixed-rate debt. Right now, you hold $20 million in 30-year 6.5 percent loan assets that were funded by issuing $20 million of 30-year 5.5 percent bonds. Your interest-rate risk is minimal. And your profit—the difference between the loan income and bond payout, or $200,000 annually— is steady.

A company shakeup, though, brings to the fore less prudent managers, who want their profits big rather than steady. One way to satisfy them is to make earnings more interest-rate sensitive by unbalancing the sensitivities of your assets and liabilities. You can do this with an interest-rate swap.

The side of the swap you take will be determined by the direction you think rates are headed. If you believe they are going higher, you'll choose the pay-fixed leg; if lower, the receive-fixed one. The notional amount in each case would equal some portion of your $20 million loan principal—the surer you are about the rate direction, and the more of a gambler you are, the larger the portion. Because swaps, unlike securities, are not accounted for in the company's books as assets or liabilities, this procedure is known as off-balance-sheet restructuring.

Your financial gurus are predicting rapidly rising rates. So you do a two-year swap, agreeing to pay fixed 6 percent sa interest on a notional principal of $5 million, with semiannual reset and payment dates. Ignoring day-count differences, the company's six-month net could now be represented schematically as $100,000 + (Libor – 6 percent) ($2.5 million), where $100,000 is half a year's profit from the company's loan business, 6 percent is the swap coupon, and $2.5 million is half the notional principal.

Obviously, this arrangement will periodically enhance or erode the company's profits, depending on whether Libor for that payment period is higher or lower than 6 percent. In a time of positive yield curves, six-month Libor will probably start out lower than the swap coupon, which is tied to the two-year Treasury. Say Libor stands at 5.8 percent during the first period—the company net for those two quarters is trimmed to $95,000. On the next reset date, however, the index has climbed to 6.2, and profits swell to $105,000.

That leaves your company right where it would have been without the swap for the first year. But if Libor continues to rise, so do your profits—by $250 per basis point.

The Good, the Bad, and the Ugly

SO IF YOUR FINANCIAL strategy includes arbitrage or hedging or speculation, a swap is one of the tools you could consider to implement it. But is it the best one? How does it stack up against alternatives in terms of cost, benefits, and how much you stand to lose if it goes wrong?

In all the applications discussed, the role of the swap could be filled by other transactions. In arbitrage, the swap replaces a simple bond purchase or sale; in the hedging examples, forward agreements or futures contracts could also be used. And speculative off-balance-sheet restructuring takes the place of the on-balance-sheet buying and selling of securities.

Why would you use a swap rather than the alternatives? To answer that question, you have to review your exposures and goals; in certain situations and to achieve certain ends, swaps have compelling advantages. They also, of course, have costs and risks against which the benefits must be weighed.

Arbitrage: Appearance and Reality

SWAPS' ADVANTAGES appear most obvious in arbitrage, where the whole aim is to create a cheaper liability or more lucrative asset than can be obtained by going directly to the market. Arbitrage gains, however, are by their nature transitory; the process winds up eliminating the very discrepancies and inefficiencies it exploits.

For instance, as more issuers discover the cost advantages of borrowing through FRNs and swapping into fixed rates, the floating market becomes saturated, driving prices down and yields up. Meanwhile, the fixed market moves in the opposite direction under pressure from investors bidding for a dwindling supply of new issues. The result is an equilibrium that leaves little margin for arbitrage profits. In the same way, currency swaps should reduce disparities among national markets—though, since such disparities often have less rational sources, such as politics, they may be more persistent.

ALL-IN COST In any case, if you spot what appears to be a perfect situation to arbitrage with a swap, look more carefully. The advantage you think you see over a simple security sale or purchase may disappear once you factor in all the costs, risks, and benefits of the various transactions involved.

Take the new-issue example: swapping seemed to

save both R&B and Classic 25bp over straight market issuance. But that calculation didn't figure in the two companies' costs for floating and administering the bond issues or the administrative expenses and dealer's spread on the swap, all of which could eat into those 25bp. Such expenses are factored into **all-in cost**, the discount rate that equates the present value of a strategy's costs with its revenue. This measurement provides a better basis for comparing alternative strategies.

OTHER CONSIDERATIONS Even if a swap's all-in cost is lower than that of straight bond issuance, the savings realized still have to be weighed against the added credit risk involved as well as qualitative differences between the two strategies. Credit risk exists for you as the end user of a swap because of the chance that the intermediary will default. This chance may appear slim, since market makers tend to be highly rated institutions. To some extent, however, you're exposed to the credit of your intermediary's other counterparties: if enough of these were to default, it might not be able to make payments to you. And if your swap was part of a new-issue arbitrage, you could be left with debt in a form you didn't want, priced at, rather than below, market. The swap dealer's quote already reflects its perception of the difference between its creditworthiness and yours. But you might assess the risk you run differently, and so wish to shave a few more basis points off your arbitrage savings.

That leaves qualitative differences. These are generally less easily quantifiable, including such factors as the two strategies' tax consequences, their status on or off the company's balance sheet, and the timing and variability of their cash flows.

Similar considerations apply to asset swaps. In the example given earlier, the investor swapping undervalued corporate paper into a floating rate needs to factor in the cost of buying the securities and maintaining the swap, as well as the swap's credit risk. Also at issue is the *securities'* credit risk, which is compounded by the swap: if the issuer defaults, the investor is out not only the bond coupon (and possibly principal) but also the swap payments that the bond income was supposed to cover. Finally, since such swaps usually involve underlying assets that, like the corporate paper in the example, have little liquidity, the investor can't easily close out the position if need arises. All these factors could well reduce the value to the investor of the synthetic asset's high yield.

On the other hand, even with their cost and profit advantages trimmed, swaps have other qualities that may make them more attractive than alternatives. For one thing, they are easier to terminate or reverse than a bond issue. Say R&B, seeing rates fall, begins to believe that floating-rate funding is the way to go after all, at least for a while. If the company had gone the straight-issuance route, it would have to redeem its bonds (assuming they contained a call provision allowing this) and fund the buyback with new short-term loans or notes. As it is, though, all R&B needs to do is terminate or reverse (see below) its pay-fixed swap and—voilà—floating-rate debt.

Hedges: The Real Thing

WITH MARKETS BECOMING more efficient, some appealing arbitrages may be more illusory than real. But how about hedging?

This also involves expense. In addition to the opportunity loss, discussed earlier, there's the cost of the hedging instrument—the execution, care, and feeding of the swap, for instance. But the advantages of hedging are very real and, unlike those of arbitrage, not attenuated by market integration and globalization. By removing some uncertainty from your company's cash flows, a hedge can reassure lenders and so lower your borrowing costs. Moreover, reducing risk also reduces the size of reserves necessary to cushion against it, thus freeing up capital for other uses.

Swaps, however, aren't the only hedging strategies available. In principle, the bank with the asset-liability mismatch could have solved its problem by buying FRNs whose payments would more or less offset the interest due on its deposits. Or it could have bought a series of consecutive interest-rate futures contracts or forward-rate agreements ("strips"), structuring the purchase so that each contract covered an interest period; then, should the short-term rate rise, the profit earned on the future or forward for that period would offset the bank's higher interest cost on its deposits.

Similar alternatives are available to hedge currency- and commodity-risk exposures. The question is, do swaps have any advantage over them?

Clearly, the bank in the example would prefer swapping to buying a new FRN. For one thing, the swap involves no transfer of principal. So it doesn't tie up a chunk of capital, and its credit risk is limited to the future value of the difference between the fixed- and floating-rate payments. It's also easier to match deposit payment dates with those of a swap than those of an FRN. Moreover, a swap, unlike an asset purchase, is usually accounted for off the balance sheet, so it doesn't disrupt financial ratios, such as debt-to-equity or fixed charges earned.

The situation is more complicated with futures and forwards. Several factors have to be weighed in choosing between one of these and a swap. One factor is the length of time the hedge has to be effective. Futures and forwards for near delivery dates (up to one year) may be more liquid than short-term swaps; but for longer terms, swaps may have the liquidity advantage.

Another consideration is the trade-off between credit risk and administrative costs. Futures exchanges require the posting of collateral and daily settlement of changes in contract value. These measures protect market participants against defaults, but the computations involved also increase overhead, and settlements can significantly affect cash flow.

The most obvious advantage of the swap strategy, though, is its flexibility. In the case of the interest-rate hedge, the bank can specify the index, payment periods, and reset dates that most closely match its deposit liabilities. In commodity-price hedging, flexibility can be even more important, since futures contracts are not available for certain products, such as jet fuel. Airlines trying to stabilize their jet-fuel expenses with futures might thus have to use heating-oil contracts, even though the two commodities' prices don't always move in tandem. In a swap, however, they could construct the floating index to parallel their actual fuel expenses.

Speculation: Real Good or Real Ugly

IN CONTRAST TO HEDGING, speculation is an unbalancing act: The speculator throws a financial structure into a disequilibrium that, in a particular situation, should result in increased profits. In the mortgage company illustration, the situation is rising short-term rates. To profit from this, the CFO increases the interest-rate sensitivity of the company's liabilities while decreasing that of its assets.

Using a pay-fixed swap to accomplish this rather than actually refinancing and selling and purchasing securities has several advantages. First of all, the swap is cheaper to execute, since it involves fewer transactions and so lower transaction fees. Moreover, the restructuring it effects is temporary—as is, presumably, the situation it exploits. When the swap matures, the original, profitable structure is restored automatically; such a restoration using the other method would involve more expensive issuing, selling, and buying.

Second, the swap may be less risky than a note purchase: A default by the note issuer reduces the income the company uses to pay its debt interest; default on the swap cancels the company's own swap obligation, leaving it just where it was before the transaction.

That isn't to say that speculative swaps carry no risk. They do, and it can be considerable, particularly if leverage is involved.

Leverage is a way of multiplying the effect of a small change in some financial variable, such as interest rates, on an investment without increasing the amount of capital involved. In the speculation illustration presented above, the mortgage company's two-year pay-fixed asset swap was on a notional principal of $5 million. This increased its semiannual profit by $250 per bp rise in Libor above 6 percent. To boost profits further, the company could enhance the effect of the Libor rise by increasing the notional principal. If, for example, it converted the entire $20 million of the bank's mortgages to a floating-rate asset, its half-year net would increase $1,000 for every basis point above 6 percent.

But what if the financial gurus guessed wrong, and rates fell instead of rising? Every bp drop beneath 6 percent would reduce profits by the same amounts. And should Libor unexpectedly take a real dive— below 2 percent for a $5 million principal; below 5 percent for $20 million—the company would have a net outflow instead of income from its investments.

Moreover, there's no reason (beyond prudence) to stop at $20 million—nothing really ties the swap principal to the actual asset amount. It could be very tempting to double it, say, to $40 million. That would raise swap profits to $2,000 per bp.

Losses, of course, would mount just as quickly, and the Libor threshold at which the transaction just breaks even would rise to 5.5 percent.

CORRECTIVE SURGERY When a financial situation turns against a swap, a speculator can stanch the capital outflow by unwinding the transaction. This is accomplished by reversing, terminating, or assigning it.

An **assignment** is a sale in the secondary market. Seeing rates begin to fall, for example, the mortgage company could assign its pay-fixed swap to a third party willing to take over its position. Since the swap's fixed coupon is higher than that available on new contracts, the company would have to offer the assignee an inducement: a lump sum equal to the present value of the difference between the original and new swaps' remaining fixed payments.

The viability of an assignment, however, depends on two conditions: First, the secondary market for the swap must be large enough so that the seller can find a buyer easily and doesn't have to take an incommensurate loss; this, in turn, may depend on how plain-vanilla or customized the swap is. Second, the transfer must be approved by the assigner's counterparty. Since the counterparty usually gains little if anything through the transfer and may lose much in the way of credit quality, approval is far from automatic. In fact, assignments are explictly prohibited in the standard swap agreement, except in certain specified circumstances (*see Chapter 3*).

An alternative would be a **reversal**, entering into another swap that is as close as possible to a mirror image of the first. In this case, the mortgage company would have to find a counterparty willing to pay a fixed rate for a period approximating the amount of time left in the original swap's tenor. A perfect match is probably impossible. The company might have to agree to receive the new, lower swap rate, which will not quite cover its fixed payments under the original contract. Or it could persuade its new counterparty to pay the above-market 6 percent by offering it an up-front payment equal to the lump-sum inducement in the assignment scenario.

IGNORANCE IS NOT BLISS So, even if you take the losing side of a speculative bet, you don't have to break the bank, literally. But there are two prerequisites to unwinding a swap successfully: First, you have to understand the connection between the economic climate and the profits and losses generated by the transaction; second, you have to know when it's time to cut and run. Basic as this may sound, press reports indicate that in the most notorious recent cases of swaps losses—Orange County, Procter & Gamble, and Gibson Greetings, for instance—one or both of these conditions may have been missing.

Quantifying probable responses to different economic situations is difficult enough for the layman when the instrument involved is something as relatively straightforward as a Treasury bond. The complexity of many modern investments and strategies compounds the difficulty: just try figuring the up- and downsides of an **indexed amortizing swap**, in which the notional principal is depleted over time according to a schedule tied to the level of some index. To make matters worse, swaps are often packaged with other instruments in **structured notes**. These can very well look like bonds to an investor, who might therefore misjudge their volatility or liquidity.

So what do you do? First, don't assume that a counterparty or swap dealer will warn you of all a transaction's potential risks. In August 1995, six Wall Street industry groups and the Federal Reserve Bank of New York, responding to regulators' concerns about the derivatives industry, issued trading guidelines that boil down to a modified caveat emptor. These were distilled in October into a generic disclaimer to be sent to clients, advising them that securities firms are not bound to advise them on their holdings when selling complex derivatives.

That means it's up to you to assure that your company has the proper mechanisms, either internal or in the form of outside consultants, to evaluate transactions for both price and risk. And evaluation has to be done not only before consummation but also periodically, throughout a swap's tenor (*see Chapter 3*).

Even an expert understanding of an instrument's risks, however, won't stave off disaster if you don't have a stop-loss policy. Knowing when to hold and when to fold was an issue long before Kenny Rogers stopped shaving. But in the age of leverage, it's particularly acute. At some point you have to admit that the economy isn't going to cooperate with the scenario underlying your financial strategy. Otherwise you'll be riding the rapids of red ink to bankruptcy.

Conclusion

SWAPS ARE POWERFUL TOOLS with applications in many facets of financial management. They're not, however, the only ones nor, in all circumstances, the best ones. You have to consider and compare the benefits, costs, and risks of the alternatives. But once you've determined that a swap is the way to achieve your company's goals, what do you do? That's the subject of the next chapter.

THE LIFE CYCLE OF A SWAP

GETTING DOWN TO THE NUTS and bolts: How do you actually do a swap?

A swap involves multiple tasks that call upon multiple skills and types of knowledge—from corporate financial strategy to accounting to jurisprudence. How you distribute the duties will depend on your company's structure and areas of expertise. You may even find it most efficient to delegate the entire process to an outside consultant specializing in such transactions—your bank, law firm, or accountants can probably make recommendations, or you might discover candidates at conferences or cited in articles on subjects like risk management.

Then again, you may feel you need help only with certain facets, such as analyzing your company's needs and creating a strategy to meet them. This can sometimes be provided by the counterparty-advisory groups that have been created within certain investment banks; some will even give you access to their risk-management systems. (Be wary, though, of possible conflicts of interest.)

Whether you handle the process in-house or shop it out, however, you should understand how it works—the responsibility, if you are an executive, is ultimately yours. It helps to think of the swap process as a life cycle comprising conception, birthing, maintenance, and maturity or death. This chapter provides brief descriptions of each stage, together with some first-hand views.

Conception:
Swaps' Place in an Overall Strategy

THIS FIRST STAGE belongs to the realm of financial management, and a detailed discussion lies far beyond the scope of this book. In brief, what's needed is a thorough study of your company's exposures and funding and income needs, the results of which provide the basis for setting goals for risk control, borrowing costs, and returns on assets. You also have to decide how much you're willing to pay to attain these goals.

When all that is done, you must choose your weapons. Swaps are just part of a large financial arsenal, including futures, forwards, options, and simple securities transactions. Even among swaps, there are several varieties (*see Chapter 4*). You have to determine which instruments or combinations of instruments suit your aims, taking into account such factors as all-in cost, cost-effectiveness, risk, flexibility, liquidity, and anonymity. Before committing to one strategy, make sure you can answer such questions as: Under what circumstances will that strategy succeed or fail? How likely is each scenario? What's the gain or damage you would sustain if it should occur?

Birthing, Part One: A Swap Sees the Light

OKAY, YOU'VE DECIDED to do a swap and chosen the kind of swap you want to do. Now you have to find a counterparty.

Often, the counterparty will find you: A bank with which you have a relationship may come to you with a deal it feels fits your financial strategy. In a new-issue arbitrage, you might do a swap with your bond's underwriter. In other cases, you might shop around. If you're doing a U.S.–dollar interest-rate swap, you'll be able to solicit bids from a large number of commercial and investment banks, as well as nonbank financial institutions such as insurance companies. Your choice is more limited for other currencies and types of swaps. (*See Appendix C for a list of market makers.*)

> **AN EXPERT'S VIEW**
>
> Swaps are an integral part of the funding strategy of the European Bank for Reconstruction and Development (EBRD). Whenever the bank issues a bond, says funding officer **Jean-Marc Debricon**, he looks for an interest-rate and/or currency swap that will "match the coupon and result in financing at a sizable margin under six-month Libor. ... Generally, we go directly to the counterparty bringing out the new-issue deal, because there's no point going to another one and provoking a leak. [But] if it's a pure plain-vanilla issue, and if [the first counterparty] gives us a quote that doesn't seem too good, well, yes, we might try the market."

In making your decision, two major, and interrelated, considerations are credit and cost. Chapter 2 discussed a swap's credit risk: the likelihood that your counterparty might default. There are several ways of dealing with that risk. One is to set a floor on the credit rating of potential counterparties, eliminating all candidates rated lower than AA, for instance; in doing this, rely on more than one agency's ratings, and check watch lists. Another method is to dilute the risk by spreading your swap business around. A third is to require credit enhancements, such as letters of credit or collateral, from weaker counterparties.

AN EXPERT'S VIEW

"The [EBRD] has a very conservative credit policy, which means that second parties must have ratings appropriate to the maturity of the swap transaction," says **Debricon**. "Some colleagues here have been working on several ways of strengthening the credit side, notably by developing a general collateral agreement. Which means that ... each counterparty, after certain marking to market of the hedging tools, would have to put up collateral or receive collateral from the other. And that obviously would reduce exposure of one to the other."

Dealers have a fourth way to handle credit risk: they charge for it. A dealer's spread (*see Chapter 1*) is partly compensation for the credit risk it assumes from both sides in mediating the swap. In **pricing** a new interest-rate swap, for example, the dealer first calculates the fixed rate that will make the market value of the swap zero—that is, the rate at which the present value of the sum of expected fixed payments equals the present value of expected floating ones, giving neither counterparty an advantage. The result of the calculation is the dealer's midrate, from which it derives its receive-and pay-fixed quotes by, respectively, adding and subtracting the same number of basis points. How many points is determined in part by the credit rating of that counterparty; market forces, of course, also play a part.

What does all this mean for you? When you're looking for a counterparty for your swap, the quoted coupon should not be your only criterion. As with any financial transaction, other considerations can be crucial. Among them:

◆ **Credit rating** The higher your counterparty's rating, obviously, the lower the risk that it will default. Many financial institutions have created special credit-enhanced vehicles to handle their swaps.

◆ **Expertise** Many dealers are full-service and able to accommodate different types of deals. Some, however, may have more experience in one area, say the U.S., than another, like Continental currencies.

◆ **Swap book** You can be affected by a dealer's other counterparties—if too many were to default, payments owed you might be jeopardized. A dealer that does a lot of transactions with different counterparties is able to offset and spread out its risks. So you might want to know the extent of its swap portfolio. The newsletter *Swaps Monitor* (*see Appendix B*) publishes a list showing the notional size of the main dealers' books.

Birthing, Part Two: Making It Legal

COUNTERPARTIES TYPICALLY conclude their transactions orally, later confirming the terms—swap coupon, index, and tenor, for example—in writing. Finally, a legal document, often incorporating the written confirmation, is drawn up and exchanged.

This document is generally based on one of the standardized master agreements developed by the International Swaps and Derivatives Association: the **Interest Rate Swap Agreement** and the **Interest Rate and Currency Exchange Agreement**. A master agreement governs all swaps in effect between one set of parties, with each transaction after the original treated as a supplement. The ISDA forms have two main parts: the text of the basic provisions and a schedule designed to permit completion and modification of these provisions. You may want to negotiate simplifications of, as well as additions to, the terms. Many standard provisions may have nothing to do with you. On the other hand, you may want to clear up certain points that are not covered. For instance, in a new-issue arbitrage, you, as borrower, might want to insert a clause making the swap conditional on successfully closing the issue, though your counterparty might object to this transference of risk.

AN EXPERT'S VIEW

In the Interest Rates and Derivatives department of Key Capital Markets Inc. in Seattle, VP **Elizabeth Romney** arranges straightforward interest-rate swaps with middle-market corporations (between $10 million and $100 million in sales) that transform floating-rate loans to fixed-rate obligations. "All of our transactions are done on ISDA master agreements," says Romney, though "we do have very simple documents, as do most banks, that we'll use if it's a [simple hedge]—just a two- or three-page agreement."

Among the issues covered in the swap contract are events of default and termination, as well as how to determine indemnification should any of these occur (more on compensation below). An event of default is a circumstance, action, or failure indicating that one party has a credit problem; at this point, the non-defaulting counterparty can end prematurely all the swaps governed by the master agreement. Bankruptcy is the obvious case. But once the protection of Chapter 7 or 11 has been invoked, the nondefaulting counterparty may have difficulty getting full compensation. For that reason, some of the default events specified in swap agreements are signals that problems may be looming—missed payments on this or other transactions, for instance—rather than actual failures.

In contrast, termination events are "no-fault." These are generally occurrences, beyond the control of either party, that make it impossible or much more expensive or a lot riskier for one or both to continue with the swap—for example, changes in the original legal, regulatory, tax, or credit situation. Which party may initiate an early termination, and how many of the swaps governed by the agreement are affected, vary with the particular circumstances.

Maintenance

AN EXPERT'S VIEW

"A separate team [puts] these deals into the system," says **Debricon**. "We don't do it ourselves, of course. And they keep tracking them for the rest of their lives—together, of course, with the controllers and auditors."

NOW THE PAYMENTS BEGIN. This entails back-office labor. In an interest-rate swap, for instance, the index must be checked on each reset date and the new value used to determine the net settlement amount and whom it goes to, all of which has to be confirmed with the counterparty. On the following payment date, the back office also has to arrange for the actual transfer of funds to and from the correct accounts. In addition, both the notional principal and the interest payments must be accounted for in the company's books (*see the* **ACCOUNTING** *entry in Chapter 4*).

Another back-office function is monitoring. The importance of this process was underlined by the Securities and Exchange Commission's November 1995 order finding Gibson Greetings remiss in not having the proper systems and procedures to account for, report, and measure the risks of their derivatives holdings. What are the proper procedures?

In 1993 the Group of 30, an international bankers' think tank chaired by former Federal Reserve chairman Paul Volcker, attempted to calm public and official fears about derivatives by issuing guidelines for controlling their risks. Taken together, the G-30 recommendations, contained in a report entitled "Derivatives: Practices and Principles," constitute a monitoring system. This entails formulating capital and risk-management policies, including credit- and **market-risk** limits; creating independent units to ensure compliance with those policies; instituting procedures and models for regular **marking to market** and stress testing under multiple scenarios; and establishing channels for quick and accurate risk reporting to management.

AN EXPERT'S VIEW

Reuters has strict guidelines on derivatives activity, requiring that no swap exceed the underlying cash investment. "We can never be more than 100 percent hedged on our interest-rate exposure," **Philip Wood**, deputy financial director, explains in an August 1995 interview for *Risk* magazine. No principal is ever at risk. "You're merely getting a different yield on the money you have," Wood adds.

The monitoring system must be sophisticated enough to track all the essential variables that determine the risks inherent in particular situations, but simple enough for nonquants to use to produce information that decision makers can understand and act upon. Though specialized swap-control software is available, this may be an area where consultants can help.

Monitoring risk limits is a back-office function. What

to do if they're exceeded is a policy decision. Management may decide to stop swap activity or curtail any further transactions with a particular counterparty. It could also unwind the swap or simply decide to institute or raise collateral requirements.

> ### AN EXPERT'S VIEW
>
> "The extreme reaction would be to say that we can't deal with you anymore because our credit to you is too big, and we don't want to increase it any more," says EBRD's **Debricon**. "Before that, of course, you have all kinds of compromises, like agreeing on the installment of some kind of collateral agreement. And this has proved quite useful."

The End

MANY SWAPS JUST PASS away quietly on their predestined dates. In these cases, you don't have much to do except compute and make the last payments and determine if a new swap is in order. A few transactions, however, meet their fate prematurely. And these can be a bit messier.

The culprit may be one of the termination or default events specified in the swap agreement. Or the counterparties may just agree to part ways because the conditions that made the swap favorable or necessary have changed.

> ### AN EXPERT'S VIEW
>
> "If we see that the bond [issued by the bank], for whatever reason—because the market is going down—is trading at very cheap levels," says **Debricon**, "we will try to buy it back and thus terminate the hedging swap."

Even if a swap is ended by mutual agreement, an

early termination entails an additional chore: determining who owes whom how much. One or both counterparties may be due payments from the last payment period, or be entitled to portions of the next scheduled payment, prorated up to the termination date. In addition, one party will also probably be owed compensation for losing a valuable asset.

As mentioned above, a swap is constructed so that its market value at inception is zero—the present values of the anticipated income streams from the two legs are equal. But as time passes, conditions change, and one leg generally becomes more valuable than the other. For instance, in an interest-rate swap, rising rates will increase the value of the pay-fixed leg while decreasing that of the receive-fixed flows. In this situation, a default would hurt the fixed payer, who would have to pay a new counterparty to take over the receive-fixed side on the original swap terms.

The counterparties to a terminated swap have to determine which of them is sustaining the loss, often referred to as "loss of bargain," and compute a reasonable compensation. In principle, three methods for doing this exist: indemnification, formula, and agreement value. In practice, though, almost everyone uses the last method, so only that will be described.

In the agreement value method, dealers (at least three, if possible) are asked what up-front payment they'd require or be willing to make to take over one side of the swap for its remaining life. Their quotes are averaged to arrive at the compensation due the counterparty that would have to pay to replace the swap.

For more unusual or customized transactions you may be able to find few dealers able or willing to quote prices; and those quotes you get may differ significantly. This was illustrated in August 1995 when Canadian insurer Confederation Treasury Services Ltd. defaulted on a long-term currency swap (with a maturity well over 10 years) with Enron Corp., the Texas energy company. Confederation claimed it was owed more than $9 million in the termination, while Enron put the number at $4.7 million; the difference reflected widely varying evaluations by traders.

Even for simple swaps, however, complications can arise when the termination is brought on by a default event. Two complicating factors are bankruptcy and limited two-way payment provisions, or LTPs.

An institution declaring bankruptcy is generally protected against the claims of creditors. In the case of a swap, this would mean that the nondefaulting party would lose not just the payments it was due under the agreement but also compensation for loss of bargain and, probably, any collateral that had been posted to protect against just such a risk. The Financial Institutions Reform, Recovery and Enforcement Act of 1989 and a 1990 amendment to the U.S. Bankruptcy Act addressed this problem by exempting swap contracts from automatic stays, allowing termination provisions to be exercised and collateral to be accessed.

More up in the air is the status of LTPs. Many contracts include one of these provisions, which state that in case of an early termination caused by a default, only the nondefaulting party is entitled to receive payments. In practice, though, because the market frowns on windfalls from exploiting an insolvency and because the legal status of these provisions is debatable, most counterparties honor full bilateral payments, even when the contract allows them not to.

Conclusion

AFTER READING THESE three chapters, you should have a good idea of what a swap is, how it could fit into your financial program, and the way in which it is implemented. Now you can dip into Chapter 4, which is arranged alphabetically, for more detailed discussions of particular topics, such as the different types of generic and nongeneric swaps.

SWAP ABCs

THIS CHAPTER IS DESIGNED for sampling. It consists of brief discussions of topics connected with swaps and their market, some of which were touched on in the first three chapters. They are presented in alphabetical order and cross-referenced, so that you can follow up easily on the subjects that interest you.

ACCOUNTING

HOW DO YOU RECORD the sums exchanged under a swap on your company's books? How do you report them, where, and to whom? How are they taxed (and when can they be deducted)? The answers to those questions are the province of accounting, a back-office function (*see Chapter 3*). Like financial management and legal review, it's an area probably best left to the experts. Specific accounting and reporting procedures for swaps are complicated, and the rules are still evolving. Broadly speaking, though, the task has three parts: accounting for the principal exchanges, accounting for the periodic payments, and reporting on both for purposes of disclosure.

A swap is not, by itself, a type of financing. So accounting practitioners generally agree that the principal involved, whether actual or notional, should not appear on the balance sheet; it appears instead as an entry in memorandum accounts in the general ledger. Swaps' off-balance-sheet status is, of course, one of their great attractions: You can use them to boost your asset income without affecting your debt-equity ratio.

In contrast to principal, periodic payments related to a swap are reflected on both the income statement and the balance sheet. The way they are reported depends on what you're doing with the swap. If you're employing it in a financing transaction—in association with a new debt issue, for example—or to hedge existing assets or liabilities, the netted swap payments may be treated as adjustments to the interest income or expense of the associated instrument, and recorded using the same method. The most common accounting method for this type of transaction is accrual, in which revenue and expense are apportioned to the periods to which they relate, regardless of when they are actually received or delivered.

If you're trading the swap, however, you have to treat it as a financial instrument in its own right, with its own value, income, and expenses. The swap's value is usually calculated by netting the present values of its expected cash flows (*see* **PRICING** *and* **MARKING TO MARKET**). The transaction must be marked to market regularly, and any change in value recognized in the income of the current period. Periodic payments, meanwhile, are recorded as revenue or expense on the income statement.

Although you don't have to record the swap principal as asset or liability on the balance sheet, you do have to disclose it. The rules for doing this are set forth in the U.S. Financial Accounting Standards Board's SFAS 105, "Disclosure of Information About Financial Instruments with Off-Balance-Sheet Risk and Financial Instruments with Concentrations of Credit Risk," and SFAS 107, "Disclosures About Fair Value of Financial Instruments." According to these standards, notes to a company's financial statement must contain the following information: the notional principal of any swaps; the swaps' nature and terms, including credit and market risk; quantification of losses should counterparties default; collateral required; concentration of credit exposure, to a particular industry, for instance; and the fair value (current market price or estimated replacement cost) of the total swaps book. Statement 119, "Disclosure About Derivative Financial Instruments and Fair Value of Financial Instruments," requires in addition a description of the company's objectives in holding the derivatives and where in the financial statements the instruments and related losses and gains are reported.

Many of these procedures may change. In November 1994, FASB instructed its staff to look for alternative ways of accounting for derivative instruments used as hedges. What it came up with was the "comprehensive income," or "realized/unrealized," approach. Basically, this would require that a company categorize its derivatives as either "held for trading" or "held for risk management." Both sets would be marked to market, but only the gains and losses of the first would be recorded on the income statement of the period in which they occur; value changes for the "risk" set would be recorded in a separate equity component on the balance sheet and not recognized in earnings until realized.

However these particular proposals fare, many FASB members believe that eventually all derivatives—except, possibly, those used for hedging nonfinancial instruments such as commodities or inventory—will be marked to market, and gains or losses recognized in income. Since this would greatly increase the volatility of recorded earnings, you might want to keep an eye on what develops. *Risk, Swaps Monitor,* and *Derivatives Strategy* (*see Appendix B*) report on FASB statements concerning swaps and other derivatives.

ACCRETING SWAPS
(*see NONGENERIC SWAPS*)

ALL-IN COST

WHEN YOU HAVE to choose among financing alternatives, one of your most important considerations is cost. This goes beyond what you pay in straight interest. For instance, new-issue arbitrage utilizing a swap will entail underwriters' fees, not to mention administrative expenses. Such factors are included in the calculation of all-in cost.

All-in cost is the converse of internal rate of return (IRR). An instrument's IRR is defined as the discount rate that equates the present value (PV) of all its future cash flows with its initial cost. All-in cost gives you the rate that, applied to future costs, equates these to initial funding.

Say you're considering financing a $10 million project. You could either issue a five-year fixed-rate bond with a coupon of 10 percent semiannual (sa) or take out a floating-rate note (FRN) at six-month Libor + 50 basis points and do an interest-rate swap, paying 9 percent sa fixed in return for six-month Libor.

On the face of it, the second looks like the cheaper alternative, by 50bp. But you haven't figured in flotation and administrative costs. Assume that the underwriting fees for the fixed-rate note and FRN are $250,000 and $275,000, respectively; that they would both cost the same $15,000 semiannually to administer; and that the swap would add on $5,000 more in semiannual administrative expenses. The all-in cost of each of the two strategies would be the discount rate that equates its future outflows (including expenses, interest payments, and final redemption) with the $10 million in initial revenue.

For the fixed-rate issuance, the equation is

$$10,000,000 = 250,000 + (1+k)^{-1} (15,000 + 500,000) \ldots + (1+k)^{-10} (15,000 + 500,000 + 10,000,000)$$

where 250,000 is the underwriting cost, 15,000 the semiannual cost of administering the bond, 500,000 the semiannual interest payment, and k is the discount rate you're solving for.

This works out to a 11.3 percent sa cost of funding. The FRN–swap equation is

$$10,000,000 = 275,000 + (1+k)^{-1} (15,000 + 5,000 + 25,000 + 450,000) \ldots + (1+k)^{-10} (15,000 + 5,000 + 25,000 + 450,000 + 10,000,000)$$

where 275,000 is the underwriting cost, 5,000 is the cost of administering the swap, 25,000 is the difference between Libor paid on the note and received under the swap, and 450,000 is the fixed swap payment.

This formula gives a cost of 10.95 percent sa. So the second strategy is indeed cheaper, though by only 35 basis points rather than 50. You might also want to adjust the figures for factors such as the credit risk posed by your swap counterparty and ease of unwinding the two positions (*see Chapter 2*).

AMORTIZING SWAPS
(see NONGENERIC SWAPS)

ASSET SWAPS

THE TERM ASSET, or asset-based, swap denotes less a type than an application or orientation: It's a swap viewed from the vantage point of an investor in an asset rather than the issuer of a liability. By combining swaps with assets, you can create new, synthetic instruments with different cash flows, or temporarily alter the flows of an existing portfolio.

There are basically two reasons for creating a synthetic asset: 1) because it gives you a better return than you could get by going directly to the market to buy an instrument with the same characteristics; 2) because you can't buy an instrument in the market with the same characteristics. Reason number one assumes some pricing discrepancy or inefficiency that you can arbitrage (*see Chapter 2*). For instance, in 1986 a large number of U.S. issuers exercised the call features on their floating-rate notes, leaving investors scrambling for call protection. One result was to drive up the price of FRNs without calls. The other was to increase the production of synthetic floaters: Investors went to the fixed-rate market—where the premium for call protection was lower—bought noncallable bonds, and did pay-fixed swaps.

Reason number two depends on market gaps, rather than inefficiencies. Take the shortage of investment-grade floaters during the 1980s, when banks, the traditional issuers, ran into financial difficulties. Investors who couldn't find high-credit-quality FRNs in the market manufactured them by buying AAA-rated fixed-rate bonds and doing pay-fixed swaps.

This same flexibility in mixing and matching issuer and cash-flow types enables you to diversify your portfolio without creating revenue-expense mis-

Diversifying with an Asset Swap

*Bond purchase and initial principal
exchange in currency swap*

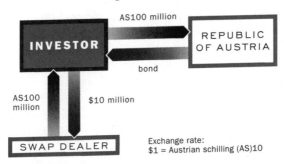

Exchange rate:
$1 = Austrian schilling (AS)10

Ongoing bond and swap interest payments

Bond redemption and swap principal reexchange

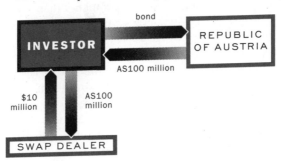

matches. Do you need floating-rate income to offset a liability? The Republic of Austria issues AAA-rated fixed 7 percent debt that you could swap into a floating rate set at a healthy margin above U.S.–dollar Libor (*see diagram on previous page*).

Conceptually, creating synthetic assets through swaps is fairly simple. Practically, though, the process is complex and risky. First, you have to deal with multiple cash flows, generated by the underlying instrument and the swap. Second, the two transactions have to be accounted for separately, which can lead to distorted reporting. Third, you're exposed to credit risk from both the security issuer and the swap counterparty. And last, unwinding the transaction can be costly, since the liquidation cost of the whole is the sum of the bid-offer spreads on each of its parts. For these reasons, all but the most sophisticated investors usually buy their synthetic assets prepackaged by financial engineers, in the form of securitized asset swaps (*see* **STRUCTURED NOTES**).

On the other hand, applying an asset swap to an existing portfolio, to change its cash-flow characteristics temporarily, is an intrinsic part of many asset-liability management programs. In this context, a swap may have several advantages over the alternative of a security trade, among them flexibility and speed.

Say you manage a portfolio containing both floating and fixed assets. At a time of positively-sloped yield curves, when long-term rates are higher than short-term ones, you might want to do an asset swap on your floating notes, which are tied to the short end of the curve. Assume you do a two-year receive-fixed swap. Your FRNs will fund the floating payments you have to make. In return, you'll receive a swap coupon set at some spread to the two-year Treasury. So, in effect, you've transformed your FRNs into higher-yielding two-year bonds. If the yield curve were inverted, of course, you'd do the opposite. Either way, a swap is much quicker and cheaper to initiate and unwind than a portfolio restructuring involving the sale and purchase of the requisite types of securities. (Note that the same transaction could be viewed as a liability swap. That is, you could be seen as taking advantage of the positive yield curve to lower your funding costs by swapping to pay the lower floating rate, using the fixed swap coupon to offset your bond-interest payments. That's what was meant by "asset swap" being an orientation.)

This is basically the tack taken by Reuters deputy financial director Philip Wood. In an article in the August 1995 issue of *Risk*, Wood explains that one way he boosts his company's returns is to "manage the yield curve" with floating-to-fixed swaps, often with deferred starts (*see* **NONGENERIC SWAPS**). He estimates that this tactic netted Reuters £61 million more in the 1992–94 period than the company would have earned on straight three-month deposits. (Of course, this reward comes with added interest-rate risk.)

In some cases, the alternative security transaction may be impossible because of legal or regulatory strictures. When Transamerica Corp. owned insurance brokerage Fred S. James, for instance, state regulations limited the instruments in which a broker could invest premiums it had collected but not yet turned over to the insurer. These instruments had to be highly liquid and placed with local depositaries. As a result, James held, on average, $100 million in short-term investments whose yield was indexed to the federal-funds rate. Transamerica couldn't trade these notes for longer-term bonds to boost yields. So instead it did a two-year swap on a portion of the principal, receiving the relatively high fixed coupon in return for Libor.

As long as the yield curve was positive, this transaction had the desired effect of increasing income. However, it also exposed Transamerica to the risk of a serious mismatch developing between the federal-funds rate, which determined its interest income, and Libor, to which its swap payments were indexed (*see* **RISK**).

ADJUSTMENT SWAP Asset swaps change the nature of a security's cash flows; an adjustment swap "adjusts" their amount or timing. For example, an investor, often for tax or accounting reasons, may use one of these transactions to transform a premium or discount bond into a par bond, or a zero-coupon instrument into one with a regular fixed coupon. In general, this adjustment is effected by means of either an up-front or a back-ended payment, made to or by the counterparty.

Satyajit Das, in *Swap and Derivative Financing* (see *Bibliography*), presents the following example of a simple adjustment swap used to transform a discount bond paying Libor flat into a par bond paying a margin above Libor. Say you buy $5 million face value of floating-rate six-month Libor notes, maturing in four years and priced at 98.8. You pay only $4.94 million, so at maturity, when the notes may be redeemed at face value, you will realize a gain of 1.2 percent on top of the Libor payments you have been receiving semiannually. But you don't want to wait until maturity for that extra 1.2 percent. Instead, you'd like to realize it as an annuity, spread out over the life of the notes. You can do this with a floating-floating adjustment swap on a notional principal of $5 million: First, you give your counterparty an up-front sum of $60,000 (1.2 percent of $5 million), which brings your investment up to a par $5 million. Then, for the remaining term of the security, you make semiannual payments of six-month Libor in return for Libor plus a margin, which is calculated to repay you that up-front 1.2 percent payment in annuity form.

ASSIGNMENT
(see also REVERSAL)

IN AN ASSIGNMENT, you transfer your obligations under

a swap to a replacement counterparty. You might assign a swap because you have sold the asset or pre-paid the liability it was designed to hedge, or because it poses too much risk, or to realize a profit. For instance, if you're the pay-fixed counterparty in an interest-rate swap and rates fall, your position will begin losing market value, since current swaps will have smaller fixed coupons. To cut your losses you might pay someone the swap's (negative) market value to take it over. On the other hand, if you were on the receive-fixed side, your position would have a positive market value. An assignee would have to pay you this value, so an assignment would enable you to realize what would otherwise be a paper gain.

In either case, a standard swap agreement (*see* **ISDA Master Agreements** *below*) would prohibit the assign-ment without your counterparty's explicit approval. Provisions for transfers, though, can be made in the schedule attached to the agreement, where the stan-dard terms may be modified to suit particular needs and wishes of the participants. And they're allowed in the standard form without consent, if your counter-party is in default or if you are adversely affected by a termination event.

BASIS SWAPS
(see NONGENERIC SWAPS)

CIRCUS SWAPS
(see CURRENCY SWAPS)

COMMODITY SWAPS

IN A COMMODITY SWAP, at least one of the flows the counterparties exchange is related to the price of a commodity. For instance, an oil producer and an oil refiner might arrange a swap in which the producer pays the current crude-oil spot price and the refiner a fixed price, both applied to the same notional quantity of the product.

Swaps like this are used by producers and consumers, to hedge against price fluctuations in their commodities, and by speculators, to make bets on those prices. As currently structured, the transactions can't serve as arbitrage vehicles, since they don't integrate different markets by linking them in the same way that interest-rate and currency swaps do. But they can involve a number of different commodities, including metals and energy and agricultural products.

Usually, both sides of a swap are based on the same commodity, as in the fixed-for-floating swap described above. To see how a simple one works, imagine that you're the treasurer of iron producer Ferrous Bueller, which turns out an average 3.33 million pounds of the metal a month. You want to protect your profits for five years from the volatility of the market. So you find a dealer (or an iron consumer) and arrange a five-year swap on a notional 10 million (3 x 3.33 million) pounds of iron: Every quarter, you pay a floating price for the notional iron, computed by averaging the closing spot prices during the quarter; in return, you

Commodity-Price Swap Used as a Hedge

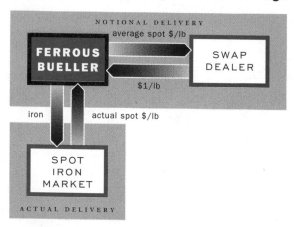

receive a fixed price of $1 a pound. Meanwhile, your company continues to sell its iron on the market, for the current spot price (*see diagram at left*).

As you can see, the payments the company gets for its iron in the market offset the floating stream it pays on the swap. Of course, the match will be less than perfect: The company receives actual spot prices and pays an average of these prices. (Some agreements use the price in effect on a particular day of the period, but averaging provides a better match to the market transactions and reduces the impact of price spikes and other temporary distortions.) Nevertheless, the swap should leave you with a fairly steady income of about $10 million to record on the quarterly financial statements.

In hedging price risk, commodity swaps function much like futures contracts. But swaps have distinct advantages, particularly for longer-term transactions. Generally, only commodity futures contracts three to six months out are liquid enough for hedging. It would be possible to use such short-term contracts and keep rolling them over, but this would require more bookkeeping and expose the hedge to a changing basis—one month, a contract might trade at a premium to the spot price; the next, at a discount.

Administering a series of futures is also more complex than administering a swap, involving an initial deposit for each contract, which is adjusted according to daily marking to market. Futures, moreover, can involve several risks: Available contracts may not match the desired product (only heating-oil futures may be available to hedge the jet fuel you use), period of coverage, delivery location, and currency. Swaps, in contrast, are easily tailored to each of these requirements.

PRICE-FOR-INTEREST SWAPS With a normal commodity swap, a producer assures a stable price for its product. A price-for-interest swap ensures the stability of the relationship between product income and financing.

Say that, to fund its operations, Ferrous Bueller took out from the bank a floating-rate loan on which it pays six-month Libor. At current rates and prices, income from iron sales easily covers the interest payments. But changes in the money and commodity markets could squeeze profits. To prevent this, you, as treasurer, might arrange to swap a fixed amount of iron (or the dollar equivalent, computed using a specified price index) for payments linked to six-month Libor.

The details of such a transaction are a bit complex. For instance, the notional principal on which the swap's Libor payments are figured would likely be calculated as follows: The amount of iron involved in the swap is multiplied by an agreed-on fixed price, and the result of this multiplication is divided by the fixed coupon for an interest-rate swap of the same maturity. This reflects the fact that your counterpar-

Price-for-Interest Commodity Swap

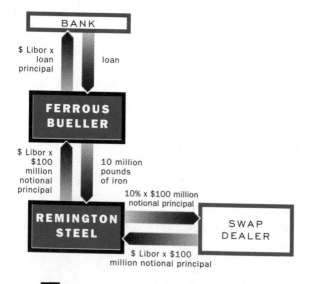

BANK

$ Libor x loan principal

loan

FERROUS BUELLER

$ Libor x $100 million notional principal

10 million pounds of iron

10% x $100 million notional principal

REMINGTON STEEL

SWAP DEALER

$ Libor x $100 million notional principal

ty in the commodity swap (a swap dealer or iron consumer) will probably hedge its position with a pay-
fixed interest-rate swap. Assume that you agree to
deliver 10 million pounds of iron each quarter to
Remington Steel Co. under the commodity swap. If
the fixed iron price is set at $1 a pound and the cur-
rent interest-rate swap coupon is 10 percent, the
notional principal for your Libor receipts will be $10
million/0.10, or $100 million (*see diagram at left*).

Note that this calculation does not refer at all to
the amount of your loan. Therefore, the Libor payments you receive under the swap may or may not
equal the interest you owe. However, the dollar difference between the two will remain the same
throughout the life of the swap. In this way, you have
effectively switched your debt payments from floating
dollars to 10 million pounds of iron (plus or minus a
set dollar sum).

Remington, meanwhile, fixes its iron costs at $1 a
pound: Its Libor outlays under the commodity swap
are completely offset by its Libor receipts from the
interest-rate swap. So, in effect, it pays for the 10 million pounds of iron it receives from Ferrous Bueller
with the $10 million (0.10 x $100 million) it pays
under the interest-rate swap.

MACROECONOMIC SWAPS If you're a manufacturer, fixed-for-floating-price commodity swaps can stabilize your expenses. But what about your income?
That depends in part on how much of your product
you sell, and unit-sales quantity may be seriously affected by the state of the overall economy. Managing the
"quantity" risk posed by larger economic phenomena,
such as business cycles and inflation, is the province of
macroeconomic hedging. One of the tools that might
be used for this purpose is the macroeconomic swap,
which made its first appearance as a hypothetical transaction proposed by J.F. Marshall, V.K. Bansal, A.F.
Herbst, and A.L. Tucker in articles published in 1992

(*see Bibliography*). Since then a limited market has developed for this variation on a commodity swap.

The "commodity" involved is an economic variable, such as consumer confidence. If your company's unit-sales numbers correlate closely with one of these variables, you might consider a swap in which the payments of one leg are linked to the level of the appropriate index.

Say you're a tour operator. It's no secret that people get wanderlust when the economy's good and hole up at home when times are bad. Looking at past years, in fact, you find that you can pretty much predict the amount of business you'll get in a particular month by looking at the Conference Board's Index of Consumer Confidence (ICC) for the previous quarter.

To even out your operations income, you might do a swap like the following: Every quarter, you pay the swap dealer a fixed 20 percent sa on a notional $250,000. In return, the dealer pays you a floating rate, based on the ICC level observed the previous quarter, applied to the same $250,000. The ICC is figured on a scale of 0 (absolutely no confidence) to 100 (perfect). So the formula determining the floating payment would be something like $(100 - ICC)/100 \times \$250,000$.

Say the index for the first period stands at 80, indicating general happiness about the economic future—the floating and fixed payments both equal 0.20 x $250,000 and so cancel each other out. But then consumer confidence falls. If it reaches a level below 80, you'll receive a flow from the swap that will help tide you over a travel slowdown. Of course, if confidence soars above the 80 mark, you'll be the one shelling out. But assuming you were right about your business's correlation with the ICC, your extra cash flow from operations will cover the swap payments.

NOTE: Hedges are only as good as the correlations they are based on. Some of these are fairly straightforward—if you hedge fixed-income instruments with a pay-fixed swap, interest-rate movements will general-ly send one up and the other down by approximately offsetting amounts. Other correlations, like the one just described, might be more tenuous, holding for certain periods and not others. If customers don't start to tour when the economic sun shines, the tour oper-ator in this example could take a beating.

CURRENCY SWAPS

A BASIC CURRENCY SWAP consists of three parts: an initial exchange of equivalent amounts of two different cur-rencies, as determined by the current spot exchange rate; periodic interest payments, generally a fixed rate in one currency for Libor in the other; and a final reexchange of the original sums, using the initial exchange rate. Say Lyonnais kitchenwares company Guillaume Napa needs capital for a new warehouse and plant. French investors, having seen GN come to market three times in the past year, are ready to shrug off a further offering; in the United States, on the other hand, bond buyers can't get enough high-cred-it Continental debt. The company can borrow more cheaply across the Atlantic. But it can't use dollars in its operations and doesn't want exposure to foreign-exchange risk. So, it does a currency swap.

First, the company floats an issue in the U.S.: $10 million of five-year bonds with a 12 percent sa coupon. Then it finds a dealer willing to pay 12 percent on $10 million, semiannually for five years, in return for six-month French franc Libor on the equivalent amount of francs.

The current exchange rate is 4 francs to the dollar. So in return for the $10 million in bond proceeds, the dealer gives GN Ff40 million, which the company uses to fund its expansion. Then, every six months for the next five years, GN pays the dealer the current Libor rate on Ff20 million and is paid $0.6 million, which it distributes to its American bond investors. Finally, at

Currency Swap Used for Arbitrage

*Bond issue and initial principal
exchange in currency swap*

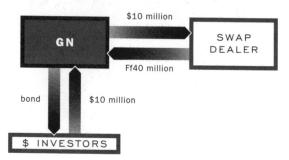

Ongoing interest payments

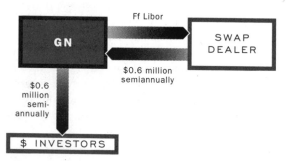

Bond redemption and reexchange of swap principal

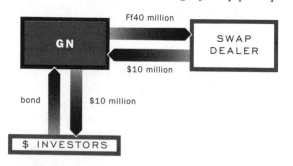

maturity, the two exchange their last interest payments and reexchange the dollar and franc principal amounts: GN gives the dealer Ff40 million + (current Ff Libor) (Ff20 million) and receives $10 million + $0.6 million, which it uses to pay off its obligation.

As the diagram at left shows, the payments GN receives from the swap completely cancel out the payments it must make on the bond, leaving the company with a pure franc obligation and no currency risk. If the swap rate had been higher than the bond rate (a not uncommon situation), GN's borrowing cost would be further reduced.

The use of currency swaps to reduce borrowing costs is common among corporations and international organizations, and has even been adopted in academia. In January 1995, for example, Harvard University sold 75 million Swiss francs ($58.25 million) of two-year notes in Switzerland, where the school's AAA rating was well received, and exchanged them for dollars through a swap with Merrill Lynch Capital Markets, a unit of Merrill Lynch & Co. The result, according to Harvard's director of financial systems, Judy Warren, was funding at a quarter percentage point less than the university could have achieved in the U.S. market.

Despite the popularity of this kind of arbitrage, though, the increasing integration of the world's markets should result in fewer opportunities. And as pointed out in Chapter 2, even existing arbitrages may bring savings that prove illusory once all the costs are factored in. On the other hand, currency swaps are definitely useful in other applications, particularly hedging currency risk.

Imagine that Springbok, a sneaker company based in Munich with global outlets, has on its books a $10 million 10-year 7 percent bond it issued three years ago in the U.S. market. Every six months, it has to pay its American bondholders $0.35 million in interest,

Currency Swap Used as a Hedge

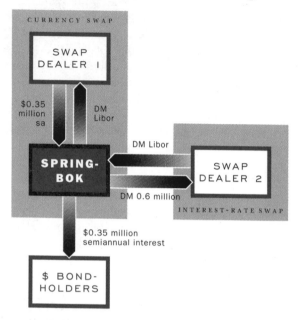

but most of its income is in deutsche marks. So far this mismatch hasn't been a problem, but now the strengthening dollar has Springbok's treasurer worried. Foreign-exchange futures and forwards contracts won't work to hedge the seven years remaining till maturity. So she decides to do a dollar-mark currency swap.

She finds a dealer who agrees to pay 7 percent sa on $10 million, semiannually for seven years, in return for DM Libor on the equivalent amount of deutsche marks: DM20 million, at the current rate of 2 marks to the dollar. Unlike in the basic currency swap, however, these principal amounts are exchanged only at maturity.

The swap transforms the company's fixed dollar liability into a floating deutsche mark one, eliminating currency risk. But the treasurer doesn't like the rate uncertainty created. So she tacks on an interest-rate swap, paying a fixed 6 percent sa in return for DM Libor, both applied to a notional DM20 million. The final structure is known as a "circus swap": two fixed-floating swaps in which both floating legs are tied to Libor. The result, as the diagram at left shows, is a fixed $–fixed DM swap.

In reality, the treasurer might have a harder time: Par swap rates may well be below 7 percent. So, if she wants to cover the interest payments on the U.S. bonds completely, she'll have to do an off-market swap, paying either a lump sum up-front or a margin over Libor for the life of the swap, to make the cash flows of both legs equal (*see below, under* **NONGENERIC SWAPS**).

This example illustrates one departure from the plain-vanilla currency swap: the lack of initial exchange of principal. Similarly, the reexchange may be eliminated, though in this case one counterparty will still receive a settlement amount to account for changes in currency rates. Say that at the beginning of such a swap, $10 million was exchanged for DM20 million, implying a rate of 0.5 dollars to the mark; now, at maturity, the dollar has weakened so that it takes 0.55 to buy a mark. The counterparty who received the dollars at swap initiation gets a payment of $1 million at the end, since that's what he would have realized on a principal reexchange (he'd return $10 million, but the DM20 million he got back would be worth $11 million). Other variations include the floating-for-floating and the fixed-for-fixed swap, each of which may be accomplished either through a single transaction or through two, as above.

EQUITY SWAPS

LIKE MACROECONOMIC SWAPS (*see* **COMMODITY SWAPS**), equity swaps also use indexes, but to simulate exposure to a market rather than to provide a hedge against quantity risk. Structurally, one leg's payments are determined by an index, such as the Standard & Poor's 500, and the other's by a fixed or floating interest rate. Say you're a portfolio manager with a large, broad-based equity holding. You foresee a period of general stock-price volatility and you want to ensure that, for this period, your portfolio earns a certain minimum return. You could sell shares and buy bonds. But that's a pretty expensive solution to what you see as a temporary problem. The same effect can be achieved, with less trouble and lower transaction costs, using an equity swap.

You might agree to make quarterly payments based on the total return (percent change in level plus dividends) of the Standard & Poor's 500 Stock Index in exchange for receiving a flat rate of 9 percent per annum, both calculated on an initial notional principal of $100 million. As the diagram below shows, this has the effect of transforming the volatile returns of your portfolio into a stable fixed rate.

Equity Swap

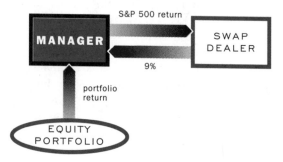

If your portfolio is less well balanced, or if you believe only one market sector is going to suffer the volatility you want to avoid, you might choose the appropriate, more narrowly defined index, perhaps the Morgan Stanley Cyclical. Another choice you have is between fixed and variable notional principal. The variable-principal alternative is used to replicate the cash flows of a direct investment in the relevant equities, assuming reinvestment of dividends. It does this by adjusting the swap principal every payment period by the amount of the equity-side payment.

Say the index-plus-dividend return on a reset date stands at 2,014, compared with 1,900 the previous quarter: The equity payment for the period is $100 million x (2,014 – 1,900)/1,900, or $6 million, and the notional principal for the following payment period will be $106 million. On the next reset date, the index-plus-dividends level is 1,984; so the equity payment will be $106 million x (1,984 – 2,014)/2014, or approximately –$1,579,000, and the principal is again adjusted, to $104,421,000. (Note that since the index return for this period is negative, you, as the equity-pay party, would receive, rather than pay, $1,579,000, added onto your normal fixed receipt.)

AN EXPERT'S VIEW

The July 1995 *SmartMoney* reported that corporate officers compensated largely with shares in their companies' stock (which many were banned from selling) were using swaps to avoid having all their eggs in one basket. It worked something like this: Say LMN VP Jan Smitts has earned $3 million in the company's stock as part of his bonus. He arranges to pay a bank all his LMN dividends, plus any capital appreciation, in return for the total return on $3 million invested in the S&P 500. In this way, Smitts effectively diversifies his portfolio, from being invested almost entirely in LMN to exposure to all the companies in the index.

Our initial example notwithstanding, most of the

natural participants in the equity-swap market are on the equity-receive side. Index-fund managers are the most obvious candidates: By applying equity-receive swaps to underlying holdings of fixed- or floating-rate bonds, they can mirror the index return exactly. And if they don't want to tie their returns to just one set of stocks, they can mix and match. In a blended swap, for instance, the equity-side payout is based on a weighted average of (usually two) indexes. In an asset-allocation swap, it is the greater of two index returns; of course, doubling your chances of winning in this way has a cost, in the form of a higher fixed coupon or an up-front payment.

A synthetic index portfolio may generate higher returns than an actual one. In part, this is because its transaction costs are lower. There are also arbitrage opportunities that can be exploited by equity swaps, particularly for investors desiring exposure to foreign markets.

For example, many governments impose a with-holding tax on dividends paid to foreigners. This amounts to 15 percent in the United States. So if you're a German investor interested in a segment of the American market whose dividend rate is 2 percent, you'd make 30 basis points more by entering it through an equity swap instead of a direct investment.

Similarly, swaps help investors circumvent the turnover taxes levied by some countries, such as the United Kingdom, and the custodial fees that banks charge for holding foreign securities. Moreover, they avoid problems with liquidity or the artificially large bid-ask spreads in some markets, as well as difficulties associated with countries' differing settlement, accounting, and reporting regulations.

ART SWAPS In principle, any product or activity with an associated price index, or for which you could create one using public information, could be the basis of an equity-type swap. That's the insight behind a recently minted swap that enables investors to gain exposure to the art market without the bother of buying, displaying, insuring, or even having to look at actual paintings and sculpture.

Art swaps, which debuted in May 1995, work like this: A dealer or fine-arts consultant creates an index based on the value of a specified portfolio of works. An individual or corporation pays the dealer a spread over Libor in return for the percent change in the index. This allows the investor to profit from rising art prices. If the index is based on a particular collection, it also allows the collector to stabilize the value of his or her artworks: The dealer passes on payments of Libor in return for the collection's price appreciation.

FORWARD (also DELAYED- OR DEFERRED-START) SWAPS
(see NONGENERIC SWAPS)

HYBRID SWAPS
(see STRUCTURED NOTES)

INTEREST-DIFFERENTIAL NOTES
(see STRUCTURED NOTES)

INDEX-DIFFERENTIAL SWAPS
(see NONGENERIC SWAPS)

INTEREST-RATE SWAP

IN A PLAIN-VANILLA interest-rate swap, the counterparties exchange periodic payments based on two different interest rates, one fixed, the other floating. In the U.S. the fixed rate, or swap coupon, is generally quoted as a spread above the most recently issued U.S. Treasury security whose maturity is closest to the swap's tenor. The floating rate, most often three- or six-month Libor, is quoted flat.

Payments are calculated by applying the two rates to

the same principal amount, which is notional. In practice, these payments are usually netted—only the difference between them actually changes hands, going to the counterparty due to receive the higher rate for that period. (*See Chapter 1 for fuller discussions of the terms and calculations involved.*)

To see how an interest-rate swap works, imagine that you're the treasurer of money-center bank Quai Corp., which has a large portfolio of floating loans indexed to prime. To fund those loans, you go to the commer-

Interest-Rate Swap Used to Hedge a Credit-Spread Mismatch

Loan and bond issue

Ongoing interest payments

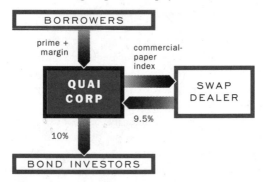

cial-paper market almost every day. This keeps your liabilities pretty much in sync with your assets—their sensitivities are similar to rising and falling rates. But you're worried about other factors that would affect your CP rate alone, such as changes in your credit quality and in investor demand.

One way to remove the uncertainty connected with these factors is to create synthetic floating debt using a fixed-rate bond and a swap. First you issue, say, $50 million of five-year bonds with a fixed coupon of 10 percent sa. Then you arrange a five-year swap on a notional principal of $50 million: You pay a floating rate based on the Federal Composite commercial-paper index in return for, perhaps, 50 basis points above five-year Treasuries (*see diagram at left*).

If the current Treasury is 9 percent sa, your funding cost is approximately 50bp over the index (because of differences in day-count conventions, the actual spread is a bit smaller; *see Appendix A*). And this spread will remain the same for the next five years, regardless of your credit rating or how blasé investors become to your offerings. (*For more on interest-rate swaps, see* **ASSET SWAPS** *and* **LIABILITY SWAPS***; for variations, see* **NON-GENERIC SWAPS**.)

INTERNATIONAL SWAPS AND DERIVATIVES ASSOCIATION (ISDA)

THE INTERNATIONAL SWAPS and Derivatives Association is a New York–based trade organization of participants in the negotiated-derivatives industry. The association developed from a small group of representatives of leading swap dealers that was formed in 1984 to standardize the documentation accompanying swap transactions. Previously, every contract might contain different terms, which not only led to costly and time-consuming legal reviews but also made it difficult to match swaps or trade them in a secondary market. In 1985 the representatives group, expanded and organized as the International Swaps Dealers Association (the present name was adopted in 1993), issued the Code of Standard Wording, Assumptions and Provisions for Swaps. ISDA revised the code in 1986 and used this version as the basis for two standard forms for swap transactions: the Interest Rate Swap Agreement and the Interest Rate and Currency Exchange Agreement, published in 1987 and updated in 1992 (see below). In addition, the association has issued various Definitions and Addenda, dealing mostly with the mechanics of payment calculation.

Today ISDA, which has some 200 members worldwide, has expanded its responsibilities beyond documentation. Its functions include representing the industry position on regulatory and legislative issues, resolving market-practice disputes, publishing market surveys, and conducting educational seminars and conferences.

ISDA'S INTEREST RATE SWAP AGREEMENT AND INTEREST RATE AND CURRENCY EXCHANGE AGREEMENT

THESE STANDARDIZED master agreements cover, respectively, U.S. dollar-denominated swaps and interest-rate and currency swaps in all currencies. Each agreement consists of two parts: a set of standard terms, with definitions, and a schedule in which these terms may be tailored to the particular needs and wishes of the two parties. As master agreements, they govern all swaps between one set of counterparties, with each transaction after the original treated as a supplement.

ISDA designed, and has refined, the two documents so that they can be adapted to almost any circumstance, at the same time defining every term to leave as little room as possible for misunderstandings or flights of fancy. As a result, it may take a specially trained lawyer to fully decipher an agreement built on an ISDA template.

The ISDA agreements are "very confusing for anyone who is not very familiar with how swaps work," says **Elizabeth Romney** of Key Capital Markets Inc. in Seattle, who arranges straightforward interest-rate swaps with middle-market corporations (those having between $10 million and $100 million in sales).

Despite their complexity, the documents governing any swaps you enter into are a must read. "The issue with the client base we deal with is almost making them read the documents. You really need to understand what you're getting into," says Romney. So here are bare-bones descriptions of some of the provisions that might concern you most.

◆ **Payments** This is probably the most important part for the majority of end users; the rest of the agreement deals mainly with what happens when something goes wrong, and with any luck, you'll never have to worry about most of the situations covered. Specifics, such as how and when a floating rate is reset and when payments are due, are contained in the schedule—but you can also find them in the confirmation, which is generally a simpler document.

◆ **Credit-support documentation** This spells out what guarantees, security agreements, or letters of credit one counterparty may require from the other before entering into the agreement.

◆ **Early termination** The agreement specifies when one party to a swap may end it prematurely, and what kind of indemnification should be made in that case. Two classes of occurrences may lead to early termination: events of default and termination events. An event of default is a circumstance, action, or failure indicating that one party has a credit problem. Termination events are generally actions, beyond the control of either party, that make it impossible or much more expensive or a lot riskier for one or both to continue with the swap.

The agreement lists standard events, but these can be supplemented or changed in the schedule. Events of default are pretty clear: Some obligation is not met—for instance, a payment is missed—either under the swap agreement or in some other regard. Termination events are trickier. They include things like changes in the law that make it impossible for one party to fulfill its swap responsibilities or new regulations that impose withholding tax on the transaction.

When an event of default occurs, the nondefaulting counterparty can end all the swaps governed by the master agreement. In a termination event, only the affected swaps are ended, and the party entitled to set the end date varies with the particular circumstances. In either case, once notice has been served, both counterparties are released from their future obligations under the swap, though a termination payment may be due one side or the other (*see Chapter 3*).

◆ **Transfers** The standard agreement generally prohibits one party from assigning a swap to another counterparty (*see* **ASSIGNMENT**). However, it does allow transfers when certain termination events occur and provides for exceptions to the general ban if the two sides wish to specify them in the schedule.

NOTE: The ISDA masters are not written in stone. Don't be afraid to modify them, and don't forget to check modifications that your counterparty introduces. As noted above, ISDA wrote these agreements to cover all the contingencies their lawyers could imagine, so you may want to cut the verbiage that has nothing to do with you. On the other hand, you might add provisions that clear up issues such as interest on late payments. Finally, don't let dealers add disclaimers that completely absolve them of responsibility for determining suitability—you don't have to give up your rights. (For more suggested modifications and tips on how to get your in-house lawyers up to snuff, see "Don't Sign That Swap Contract ...," listed in the *Bibliography*.)

LIABILITY SWAPS

AS NOTED ABOVE (**ASSET SWAPS**), the distinction between a liability and an asset swap is a matter more of orientation than of substance. It all depends on what type of instrument the transaction is associated with. In fact, when attached to a portfolio that (like most corporations') contains both assets and liabilities, the same swap can be interpreted either way. That said, most swaps seem to fall into the liability category: reducing funding costs and hedging fluctuating loan rates or raw-material prices are all liability-swap functions. Since these uses are well covered in the **INTEREST-RATE** and **COMMODITY SWAP** entries, the examples in this section will relate to asset-liability management.

Say you're the treasurer of Dowdy Chemical Co. The company is paying a 9 percent semiannual coupon on $10 million in five-year bonds it issued a year ago. Interest rates have risen considerably since then, so you're sitting pretty, with below-market debt. But you think it's about time for rates to take another dive. Can you work it so that, when they do, the company's debt will still be a good deal?

The first thing you might do is enter into a four-year swap on a notional $10 million, receiving a fixed 10 percent sa and paying Libor. This gives you variable funding at approximately 100 basis points below Libor (the margin is slightly smaller, because of day-count differences; *see Appendix A*). Then you wait for rates to fall. When they do, you reverse: You do another four-year swap, on the same notional principal, but this

Keeping Your Debt Payments Below Market

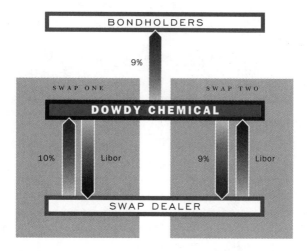

time paying fixed—9 percent, say—and receiving Libor (*see diagram*).

This transforms your debt back to fixed rate, at 8 percent (see table below). So even though rates have fallen back to where they were when you originally issued, the interest you're actually paying is still below market.

Income (+) and Outflow (–)

Bond:		– 9.0%
Swap 1:	– Libor	
		+10.0%
Total 1:	– (Libor	– 100bp)
Swap 2:	+ Libor	
		– 9.0%
Total 2:		– 8.0%

Now say you're at Bellwether Corp. The company has a policy of doing most of its funding through floating-rate loans, since this is the cheapest mode when the yield curve is sloped normally. Right now Bellwether has $200 million in notes outstanding, set at Libor plus 10bp. You'd like to lower this rate.

First, you might do a two-year swap on a notional principal of $200 million, paying 10 percent sa in return for six-month Libor. Then in six months, when the swap rate has risen (as expected with a positively-sloped curve), you reverse, receiving maybe 11 percent and paying Libor. This returns you to a floating rate, but at a margin of 90bp below Libor.

Income (+) and Outflow (−)

Bond:	− (Libor	+ 10bp)
Swap 1:	+ Libor	
		− 10.0%
Total 1:		− 10.1%
Swap 2:	− Libor	
		+ 11.0%
Total 2:	− (Libor	− 90bp)

This strategy runs more risk of loss than the first. While waiting for rates to fall, Dowdy's funding was still low, at 100bp below Libor. Between its two swaps, on the other hand, Bellwether has to shell out a fixed rate of 10.1 percent, which, given the positive yield curve, is considerably higher than the floating rate it would otherwise be paying. The longer rates take to rise, the more costly the strategy.

When a swap is used for hedging, it shouldn't really matter whether the transaction itself is profitable, as long as it reduces the risks it was supposed to. That is the position expressed by **Hans Pohlschroeder**, assistant treasurer of Colgate-Palmolive Co., in an interview with *Risk* magazine. Colgate uses interest-rate swaps to ensure that about a third of its debt in each capital market is floating-rate, a mix seen as representing the lowest cost for an acceptable level of risk. When a buyback program resulted in the floating-rate proportion rising to 44 percent, a 30-year and a 10-year pay-fixed interest-rate swap restored the balance. They also happened to make money, as the 30-year and 10-year rates fell. But, Pohlschroeder insists, that's beside the point. Once a hedge position is on, he says, it will not be lifted just to take a view on the market.

MACROECONOMIC SWAPS
(see COMMODITY SWAPS)

MARKING TO MARKET

AT SOME TIME during the life of a swap, you'll need to find out how the market would price it. In a termination, for instance, the swap's market price determines what compensation you or your counterparty will receive; in an assignment, it is the up-front payment you give or obtain. In addition, the Group of 30 guidelines (*see Chapter 3*) recommend that holders of swaps periodically price their positions to calculate their credit exposures—how much they would lose if particular counterparties should default—and to track their gains or losses on the transactions.

A swap's market price is what a dealer would pay or require you to pay to take it off your hands. Any seasoned swap is probably not par valued—that is, because of market changes, the present values of its two legs' future cash streams are no longer equal, as they were initially constructed to be (*see* **PRICING**). The market price is based on the sum necessary to rebalance the two cash streams, just like the up-front payment due in an off-market swap (*see* **NONGENERIC SWAPS**).

For liquid plain-vanilla swaps, arriving at this sum is relatively simple—as Casey Stengel used to say, you could look it up. More complex transactions, however, and those with limited markets require more sophisticated evaluation processes. Leslie Lynn Rahl, of consultancy Capital Markets Risk Advisors, suggests in a 1994 article in *Futures Industry* that you stratify your portfolio contents according to which method you use to mark them to market. This, Rahl points out, reveals how reliable your portfolio-risk assessment is by indicating how close your value estimates might be to what you'd actually realize if you had to liquidate. For example, you might divide swaps into

- ◆ simple, popular ones, for which you can obtain prices from public sources, such as newspapers and screens;
- ◆ those not quite so transparent but still widely traded, allowing you to get quotes from three dealers;
- ◆ more-tailored and composite transactions, for which no price is directly observable but that you can break into pieces similar to traded transactions, the sum of whose prices approximate the value of the whole;
- ◆ exotic transactions that you must rely on a theoretical model to price.

The higher the percentage of swaps in the first two categories, the more reliable your credit- and market-risk assessments (*see* **RISK**). Synthesizing prices takes specialized skill, and the results of marking to model reflect the biases of the model you choose.

The iffiest procedure for pricing, of course, is to rely on the dealer who sold you on the swap. If you have to do this, some experts advise, don't buy.

NONGENERIC SWAPS

FOR THE MOST PART, the swaps described under the category headings are plain vanilla, or generic. These are the simplest and often original forms. But as more participants have found more uses for swaps, almost every element of their structures has been modified—from the timing of rate setting and ending and commencement dates, to the type and speed of cash flows, to the treatment of principal.

TIMING Normally, a swap begins accruing interest at previously contracted rates within a short time after the counterparties reach agreement; it then continues until the specified maturity date (barring default or termination events). It is possible, however, to delay starts, defer rate setting, and accelerate or retard endings.

Your company, for instance, might bid on a construction project for which it will need major funding in four months. It's hesitant to go into debt until it has to, but if the yield curve steepens, waiting could be expensive. You can hedge that risk by doing a pay-fixed swap whose coupon is set now but that doesn't begin accruing interest until four months later, when you'll

Forward Swap

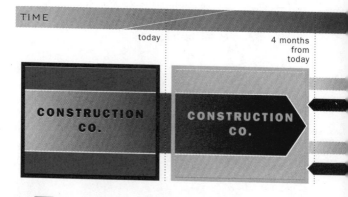

be ready to go to the market. At that point, you'll issue a floating-rate note and execute the swap, ending up with debt at an acceptable fixed rate, no matter what happens to the yield curve in the meantime.

This is what's known as a forward—also deferred- or delayed-start—swap. It allows you to lock in today a rate that you'll start paying in the future (*see diagram*).

What if you expect rates to fall, but are afraid that credit premiums will rise? A forward swap will protect you against the second eventuality, but it will also prevent you from taking advantage of the first. If, on the other hand, you wait four months and do a normal swap, you might benefit from the lower rates only to be zapped by the wider spreads. You need to be able to fix the spread now and set the reference rate sometime later, within the next four months. A spread-lock, or deferred-rate-setting, swap lets you do just that.

With a spread-lock swap, you contract to pay the current spread above Treasuries, say, 40 basis points, leaving the actual rate unspecified. When the Treasury yield for the appropriate maturity reaches a level you find attractive—7.6 percent, perhaps—you issue your FRNs and start the swap, paying an 8 percent fixed coupon.

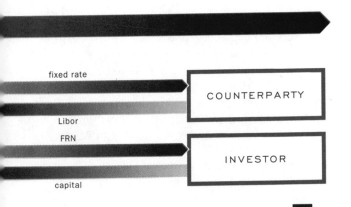

fixed rate

COUNTERPARTY

Libor

FRN

INVESTOR

capital

In addition to fixing future funding costs, forward and spread-lock swaps are used to extend existing swaps, and to coordinate portfolio-profile changes with anticipated economic movements. The same principles can be applied to currency as well as interest-rate swaps, with the added specification of the appropriate forward exchange rate.

Now consider another wrinkle in your funding scenario: Your company's bid may not win the contract. If it doesn't, you won't need the funding. And without the funding, you don't want a swap. But you're committed to doing one by both the forward and spread-lock structures. You need to have the option to take it or leave it. In other words, you need a swaption.

A swaption is essentially an option, traded over the counter, on the fixed leg of an interest-rate swap: a call, or receiver, swaption entitles the holder to receive fixed; a put, or payer, swaption, to pay fixed. To solve your construction-funding problem, you'd buy a payer swaption with an expiration date four months forward, specifying either the rate or the spread you want to lock in. If the company's bid wins, you exercise the option; otherwise, you let it expire.

This strategy raises your funding costs a bit: You have to pay an option premium equal to some portion of the notional principal, perhaps 20bp. But this buys you great flexibility.

Swaptions can lock in rates for investors as well as for borrowers. Say you hold a 10-year bond maturing in six months, and you plan to reinvest the returned principal. Right now, 10-years are paying 11 percent semi-annually, which suits you just fine. But you're afraid rates may be about to tank. You could assure yourself of getting a coupon at least as good as the current one by buying a receiver swaption with a strike of 11 percent and an expiration date six months from now. If rates stay the same or rise, you'll buy a bond in the market and let your option expire; if they fall, you'll buy a floating-rate note and exercise your option to swap it into a synthetic 11 percent fixed-rate bond.

Swaptions can also be used for pure speculation. For example, if you were pretty certain that rates were going up, you might buy a five-year payer swaption with a strike set at the current coupon for that maturity, say 8 percent sa. If you're wrong and rates fall, you're out the cost of the premium. But if rates rise—to 8.75, for instance—you make a nice profit: Once you exercise the option, you have a pay-fixed swap with a below-market coupon, which you can sell for a tidy sum. Alternatively, you can spread out your winnings by doing a reverse swap, to receive the higher current coupon, and pocket the 75bp difference every payment period. In figuring your real return, of course, you have to subtract the premium as well as the interest that money could have been earning.

Most often, though, swaptions are used to either hedge or arbitrage embedded capital-market options. Say that, as company treasurer, you decided to reduce your borrowing expense with a puttable issue, which gives holders the right to sell their bonds back on specified put dates. Investors will pay more for this feature, which protects them against loss of principal and investment opportunity if rates rise. That cuts your costs, but it also means you may have to refinance before bond maturity, at a higher rate. You can hedge this risk by buying a payer swaption with a strike equal to the bond coupon. If rates rise and investors put their bonds, you finance the buyback with floating-rate notes and exercise the option to swap them into a fixed obligation at a below-market rate.

Swaption arbitrage exploits the fact that the swap market generally assigns a higher value to options than the capital market does. This means that a borrower can lower costs by issuing a callable bond, in effect buying a call option from investors, and simultaneously selling a receiver swaption with the same strike and

Issuer Arbitrage Using a Swaption

Issue of callable bond and sale of swaption

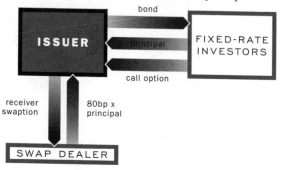

Ongoing interest payments

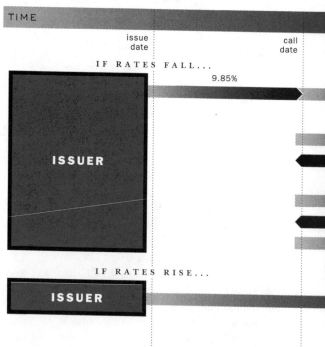

expiration. Similarly, an investor can boost returns by buying a put in the capital market in the form of a puttable bond and selling it in the swap market as a payer swaption.

For instance, if five-year bullet bonds are selling at 9.75 percent, a bond callable in three years might be priced to yield 10 basis points more, or 9.85 percent. At the same time, a two-year receiver swaption, exercisable in three years with a 9.85 percent strike, might have a premium of 80 basis points, which works out to 20bp per annum over a five-year period. So, by selling both callable bonds and a receiver swaption, a borrower can create a synthetic bullet issue at a 10bp saving over direct issuance (*see diagram*).

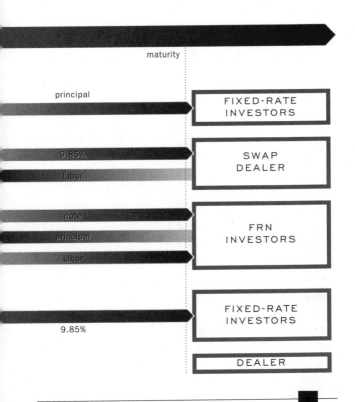

Investor Arbitrage Using a Swaption

Bond purchase and sale of swaption

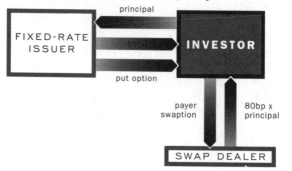

Ongoing interest payments

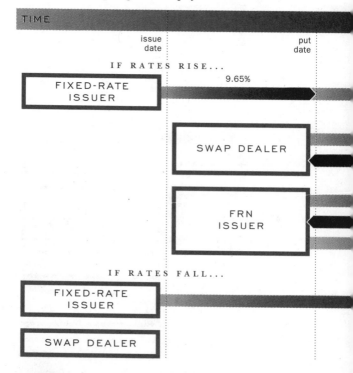

If rates remain steady or rise, neither the swaption nor the call on the bonds will be exercised. If rates fall and the swaption is exercised, the borrower will call the issue, funding its buyback with floating-rate notes whose coupon payments will be covered by the swap. In either case, it ends up with five years of fixed 9.85 percent funding (assuming that it doesn't have to pay more than Libor on the notes), which is reduced by the swaption premium to the equivalent of 9.65 percent.

In the same situation, a puttable five-year bond might yield 9.65 percent and a payer swaption with a 9.65 percent strike cost 80bp. By buying the first and writing the second, an investor could construct a synthetic bullet

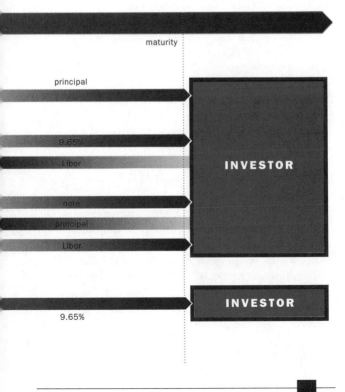

bond yielding 10bp more than the market bullet (*see diagram on previous pages*). If rates remain steady or fall, nothing happens. If they rise and the swaption is exercised, the investor puts the bond back to the issuer; the refunded principal buys a floating-rate note, whose interest income will offset the floating swap payments. In both cases, the result is a synthetic bullet bond paying 9.65 percent plus the swaption premium. This works out to 9.85 percent, compared with 9.75 percent on the bullet available in the market.

Like interest-rate options, swaptions can be embedded as well as freestanding. The nomenclature here is very variable. In the most consistent usage, a callable swap can be terminated by the fixed payer, a puttable swap by the fixed receiver. There is also an extendable swap, which can be continued beyond its maturity date at the bidding of whichever party pays for the privilege.

A callable or puttable swap is equivalent to a combination of normal one and an option on a reverse or mirror-image swap, which is exercisable sometime before maturity; exercised, the reverse generates cash flows that cancel out the original ones, effectively terminating the transaction. An extendable swap is also equivalent to a swap plus swaption. But this time the option exercise date coincides with the original maturity, and the optioned swap repeats the first one's terms over a new tenor.

In its most basic role, a callable swap allows a pay-fixed counterparty to hedge against adverse interest-rate movements and still take advantage of favorable ones. A company with floating-rate liabilities that it has swapped into fixed to match its assets might want to switch course when rates fall. A callable swap enables it to do that by just terminating the agreement. There's a cost, of course, in the form either of an up-front payment (equivalent to the option premium) or a higher swap coupon. But the alternative—doing a normal swap, then assigning or reversing if need arises—might be costlier, if not impossible.

A puttable swap gives a receive-fixed counterparty the same type of flexibility, for a similar price. An extendable swap allows the end user to benefit from conditions that favor the continuation of the swap. For instance, a company might issue fixed-rate bonds with associated warrants to issue more in the future. If the company's true preference is for floating-rate debt, it might want to do a pay-fixed swap that could be extended (probably upping the amount of notional principal, as well) in case the warrants are exercised.

Like freestanding swaptions, these embedded options can also be used to hedge and arbitrage. For instance, the issuer of a puttable bond might do a receive-fixed swap ending on the put date but extendable to the bond's maturity date should investors decide not to redeem early. Or a company might sell bonds with a call feature and do a callable receive-fixed swap, in effect buying and selling call options in the capital and swap markets, respectively. If rates remain steady or rise, the company has floating-rate debt until the bond matures; if they fall, both calls are exercised, terminating bond and swap. Because of the price disparity noted above, the premium the company pays investors for the bond call is probably smaller than the one it receives from its swap counterparty. As a result, it lowers its borrowing costs.

CASH FLOWS In the conventional interest-rate swap, one leg is fixed, the other floating. In a basis swap, both rates float, tied to different indexes, often Libor and the Federal Reserve Composite commercial-paper (CP) rate.

Basis swaps are naturals for borrowers that would prefer funding tied to one index but find it more convenient or cost-effective to borrow in another market. For instance, a European company may not want to undergo the credit rating and other processes necessary to qualify as a commercial-paper issuer in the

U.S., or it may get better terms in Libor markets, where its name is better known. If the company still wants CP-based funding, either because it holds CP-linked assets or it believes the paper rate will rise more slowly, it can borrow at Libor and swap into the CP index (*see diagram at right*).

Both borrowers and investors can use basis swaps to diversify their portfolios. Say you hold a large concentration of commercial paper. If you want to make your asset income less sensitive to changes in the CP rate, you could swap part of your holdings to a rate tied to Libor or U.S. Treasury bills.

In a variation on the basis swap, one or both legs are linked to long-term rates, reset quarterly or semiannually. For instance, you could swap six-month Libor for the 10-year Treasury yield, or the 10-year for the 30-year yield. These are called yield-curve swaps, since they are sensitive not to absolute rate levels but to the relationships reflected in the curve's shape—flat, steep, positive, inverted.

Like simpler basis swaps, yield-curve swaps can be used to diversify a portfolio. They can also be vehicles for views on future term structures. If you think the curve is going to invert, for example, with short-term rates rising above long-term ones, you might do a swap in which you receive the five-year T-note yield (probably minus a margin) and pay the 30-year.

Yield-curve swaps can function as hedging tools, as well. Say you're the treasurer of an insurance company that offers guaranteed investment contracts (GICs) whose returns are pegged to the 10-year Treasury bill. You could do a swap to receive the 10-year yield in return for six-month Libor or the 30-month Treasury yield (whichever best matched your assets), and structure it to coordinate the swap and GIC payment dates.

In another variation, the index-differential swap, the two legs are tied to floating money-market rates associated with two different currencies, but all payments

Using a Basis Swap to Obtain CP Funding

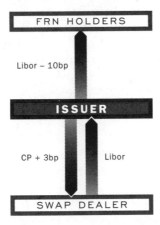

are made in one currency. In other words, you could make payments tied to U.S.$ Libor in dollars and receive payments tied to DM Libor, also in dollars.

As a borrower, you might reduce costs by issuing at a domestic floating rate and swapping to a lower foreign one, making and receiving payments only in the currency you prefer. As a speculator, you could bet on interest-rate spreads between countries, by swapping to receive a deutsche mark rate and pay a yen rate, all in dollars. As an investor, you might boost returns by buying an asset that pays U.S.$ Libor and swapping to the higher Australian-dollar rate.

Index-differential swaps (IDS) thus allow you to profit from the difference between two countries' rates without incurring foreign-exchange risk. Note, however, that currency considerations are not completely removed from the transaction. A dealer offering an IDS is exposed to both interest-rate and exchange risk, which it must hedge. The cost of that hedge is reflected in a margin added to the Libor that you, as counterparty, must pay or subtracted from the Libor that you receive.

An interesting twist is to combine an index-differential swap with a generic interest-rate swap. Say you issued a five-year floating-rate note and did a conventional interest-rate swap to convert it to a fixed-rate obligation. If the yield curve is sloped normally, the short-term U.S.$ Libor rate you receive will start out lower than the medium-term fixed rate you pay. You can narrow this difference by doing an index-differential swap to pay U.S.$ Libor in return for the higher deutsche mark rate (*see diagram at right*).

A basis swap is a variation on the generic interest-rate swap. Similar changes are rung on equity and commodity swaps. A quantro, for instance, is an equity swap in which each leg is linked to a different equity index. Say you hold a diversified portfolio of U.S. stocks but want some exposure to foreign markets. You could do a quantro, on a notional principal equal to a portion of your actual equity investment, in which you pay the total return on the Standard & Poor's 500 index and receive the return on the Nikkei 225 (*see diagram on page 104*).

In a basis-risk commodity swap, each leg is based on the spot price for a different commodity. This allows a speculator to make a bet on price spreads. For instance, if you thought fuel-oil prices were going to rise faster than those for heating oil, you would do a swap in which you received the first and paid the second.

Basis swaps depart from the *type* of cash flows associated with plain-vanilla structures. Another set of non-generic swaps vary the *speed* at which the cash flows are received: Zero-coupon swaps delay them; premium and discount swaps, also known as off-market or non-par-value swaps, accelerate them. The speed chosen may mirror the coupon structure of a security or be designed to accommodate a business's cash-flow schedule. It can also be tailored to take advantage of a favorable tax situation or to avoid an adverse one. Since tax considerations are complex, and usually peculiar to

Interest-Rate Swap
Plus Differential Swap

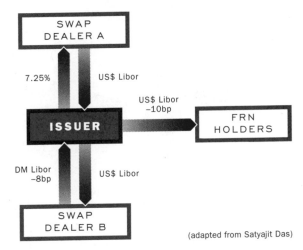

(adapted from Satyajit Das)

small groups of users or particular periods or areas, this discussion will focus on the first two applications.

A zero-coupon swap is a normal interest-rate swap except that its fixed-rate payments are aggregated into a lump sum that isn't handed over until maturity. It is thus a hedging tool for issuers of zero-coupon bonds, which take the receive-fixed side to ensure they have the cash on hand when bond-redemption time arrives. The pay-fixed counterparty, on the other hand, could well be a business trying to conserve cash flow.

Say Smithfield Holding Co. decides to take positions in three retail operations. As Smithfield's treasurer, you pay for the stock purchases by issuing a five-year floating-rate note. Normally you'd cover the interest on a borrowing with income from the asset it funded. But in this case, you can't: Your board, wishing to increase capital, plans to reinvest the dividends from these investments. Moreover, since they are growth stocks, the dividends wouldn't cover the interest due.

Quantro Swap

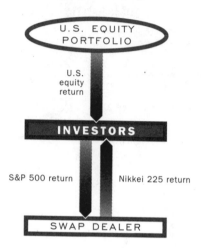

To avoid having to record negative cash flow, you might do a five-year zero-coupon swap in which you receive floating payments that offset the note's interest in return for a lump sum not due until maturity. In this way, you put off cash outflows for five years. By then, the investments should have appreciated enough to allow you to redeem the note and pay the swap interest by liquidating some of the shares. Or else dividend income from the more-seasoned companies might have grown enough to cover interest on a new note issued to cover the old debts (adapted from Satyajit Das; *see diagram on pages 106-107*).

Some general drawbacks of zero-coupon swaps: The receive-fixed counterparty sees no return on its floating payments for several years and thus takes on significant credit risk; this is reflected in a relatively high swap coupon. Meanwhile, the other side of the transaction is exposed to reinvestment risk: The end-payment calculation incorporates an assumption about the course that interest rates will take during the swap's tenor—if they are expected to rise, the lump sum must be larger, to compensate the receiver for losing the opportunity it would have had in a generic swap of reinvesting periodic coupons at the higher future rates; if the expectation is for a rate decline, the opposite is true. So interest rates that fail to rise as much as expected, or fall more steeply, shortchange the pay-fixed counterparty.

At the other end of the spectrum are off-market swaps, which accelerate their cash flows through upfront payments. A generic, or par, swap is designed so that, at initiation, its two legs' expected cash streams have the same present value. As a result, its market value starts out as zero, with neither side of the transaction owing the other money. For various reasons, however, an end user may want a swap with terms different from those prevailing in the market—a lower coupon, perhaps, or odd payment dates. In most cases, this destroys the parity of the two legs. To bring the market value back to zero, the counterparty getting the greater value has to pay the other a sum equal to the difference between the two cash streams. To the payer, this sum is a premium; to the receiver, a discount.

Off-market swaps occur in assignments (as discussed above), when new counterparties take over existing swaps on their original terms. They may also be arranged by end users with obligations that par swaps won't fully offset. Your company might have issued $20 million of 10-year 9.52 percent bonds five years ago, when its main revenues were from fixed-rate mortgages. Since then, though, its business has changed and now involves making floating-rate loans. The resulting asset-liability mismatch exposes profits to interest-rate risk, which you'd like to eliminate by swapping the bond to a floating rate. The current par coupon for a five-year receive-fixed interest-rate swap is 9.3 percent. If you're uncomfortable with the 22bp difference between this and the bond coupon, you could arrange an off-market swap, paying Libor in return for

Smithfield's Zero-Coupon Swap

Periodic payments

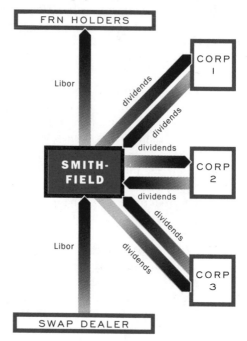

a fixed semiannual 9.52 percent. To balance the extra income you'll be getting from this deal, you would pay your counterparty a premium of $171,875.65, the present value of an 0.11 percent annuity paid semiannually on $20 million for five years, using 9.52 percent as the discount rate.

PRINCIPAL In a plain-vanilla structure, the principal—whether actual or notional—remains constant throughout the swap's tenor. But inconstancy may suit some goals better. For example, to synthesize the return of a direct investment in stocks, assuming reinvestment of dividends, an equity swap needs a variable principal (*see* **EQUITY SWAPS**).

Note redemption, final swap payment, and new note issue

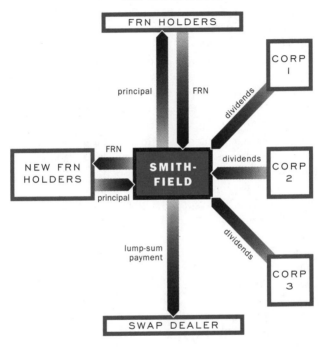

Interest-rate and currency swaps can also be constructed with principal amounts that decrease or increase over time, or do first one and then the other. These changes may occur after every payment date or following a grace period. The adjustments may be constant or graduated, or they may vary with the level of some index. The specifics are spelled out in a schedule appended to the swap agreement.

Variable-principal swaps are usually associated with assets or liabilities that behave similarly. Amortizing swaps, based on decreasing principal amounts, are often used in conjunction with amortizing loans, to change their base currency or convert them from fixed to floating or the reverse. Accreting, or step-up, swaps, whose principal increases, perform the same functions for funding facilities that involve draw-downs. And businesses with fluctuating requirements for capital might use roller-coaster swaps, whose principal rides up and down.

Imagine that your company develops office towers. Until tenants start moving in and paying rent, all your cash flow is outflow, much of it going to interest payments on floating loans used to fund the construction. You can't speed up occupancy, but you can protect yourself against rising rates by doing an interest-rate swap. The hitch is that the size of your loan liability changes with the stage of construction.

Say you have a five-year $10 million loan with quarterly payments based on U.S.$ Libor. During the 18 months of building, when you need to cover a lot of expenses, the loan principal is set to increase gradually, to $75 million. After that, it will remain steady for nine months, while tenants move in and start paying rent, and then increase by another $5 million to fund any remedial work that may be necessary. Finally, you'll start paying it down $1 million a month, making a balloon payment at maturity.

A generic interest-rate swap wouldn't fully hedge your interest-rate risk. What you need is a five-year pay-fixed swap with an accompanying schedule that specifies periodic adjustments to the notional principal that mirror the fluctuation in your borrowing. The floating receipts from this swap will now cover your loan-interest payments, and you'll be left with a five-year obligation whose cost is fixed.

Another variation on variability is the indexed amortizing swap (IAS). Here the principal decreases according to a schedule that is determined by where an index, usually Libor or a Constant-Maturity Treasury (CMT) index, stands relative to a specified "base rate."

For part of its tenor, called the "lock-out period," the

swap is an ordinary interest-rate swap, with an unchanging notional principal. After this, amortization kicks in, increasing in speed the farther the index falls. Every period, the base rate is subtracted from the index's actual level. For a negative result (meaning the index has fallen), the larger the difference, the higher the paydown; for a positive result (indicating a rising index), the paydown diminishes as the difference grows, usually slowing to zero for very large gaps. A "cleanup provision" terminates the swap prematurely if the principal drops below a certain percentage of its original size.

As an illustration, consider a swap exchanging 6.2 percent fixed for three-month Libor, with quarterly payments and resets and a $100 million initial principal. It is constructed with a two-year lock-out period, a three-month Libor base rate of 5.4 percent, a 10 percent cleanup provision, and the following amortization schedule:

3-Month Libor	Libor–Base Rate	% Reduction of Remaining Principal
2.4% or lower	–300bp	25
3.4%	–200bp	25
4.4%	–100bp	25
5.4%	0bp	25
6.4%	+100bp	20
7.4%	+200bp	7
8.4% or higher	+300bp	0

(For movements between the points on the table, amortization is calculated by linear interpolation.)

Every quarter during the first two years, the receive-fixed counterparty exchanges a payment of three-month Libor on $100 million for a flat $1.55 million. In the ninth quarter, if Libor is 8.4 percent or higher, the trade-off is the same. But if the index is lower than

8.4 percent—say, 3.4—the notional principal will decrease, to $75 million, and the payments will diminish accordingly. If Libor is still 3.4 percent the following quarter, the principal will again be reduced by 25 percent, to $56.25 million. And if, at any point, it falls to $10 million (10 percent of $100 million, the cleanup point), the swap terminates.

The end user—generally the receive-fixed counterparty—has, in effect, given the dealer a series of call options on the swap, with the base rate serving as the strike. The resulting cash flow mimics that of a mortgage-backed security. In fact, indexed amortizing swaps were created in the late 1980s as off-balance-sheet alternatives to collateralized mortgage obligations (CMOs).

Like CMOs, these swaps have attracted banks, insurance companies, and hedge- and pension-fund managers with their higher-than-market fixed rates, which are the recompense for the implicit calls. Also like CMOs, however, they carry both shortening and extension risk: If rates fall, the swap's value to the investor rises, but its life shortens; if rates rise, the swap gains in longevity what it loses in value.

Unlike CMOs, though, the swaps mitigate this "prepayment" risk through their lock-out provision, which guarantees a minimum duration. They also involve somewhat less uncertainty: IAS amortization depends solely on interest-rate movements; CMOs are affected, as well, by demographic and other factors inherent in particular mortgage pools. Nevertheless, 1995 saw plenty of red ink splattered on banks' books by indexed amortizing swaps, bought in anticipation of steady rates that didn't materialize.

NOTE: Variations, like variety, may be the spice of life. They certainly add flexibility to swaps. But they also make pricing and assessing risk more complex— the further a swap veers from the plain vanilla, the harder it is to get quotes from published sources or dealers. So, before you do a nongeneric swap, make sure you really understand its fair value and profit and loss characteristics.

PAR SWAP

THE COUPON OF A PAR, or at-market, swap is set at the current market rate. Since this rate is chosen to make the present values of both legs' future cash streams equal, neither party needs to be compensated with an up-front payment. (*Compare* **Off-Market Swaps**, *under* **NONGENERIC SWAPS**.)

PRICE-FOR-INTEREST SWAPS
(see COMMODITY SWAPS)

PRICING

"PRICING," AS APPLIED TO interest-rate swaps, denotes the process of associating a coupon with a cash value: given one, you derive the other. The cash value of a new par swap, by definition, is zero, so pricing it entails solving for the appropriate fixed coupon. For a non-par swap, either existing or new, the reverse is true: The coupon is specified in the contract, and it is the transaction's dollar value that must be found.

Both derivations involve technical issues, and a full discussion of them—as of accounting and financial management—is beyond the scope of this guide. What follows is just a sketch of the general principles, intended to help you understand the logic behind dealers' quotes on new swaps and your back office's valuations of ones already in your portfolio. For simplicity, the presentation focuses on plain-vanilla interest-rate swaps, but the process is easily extended to other types. (For more detailed but still readable accounts, see "A Blueprint for Valuing Interest-Rate Swaps," by Joel B. Finard, and *Understanding Swaps*, by John F. Marshall and Kenneth R. Kapner, both listed in the *Bibliography*.)

The pricing of an existing swap (**MARKING TO MAR-**

KET) is the less complex task. Essentially, it consists of deriving the present values (PVs) of both legs' remaining cash flows and subtracting one from the other; the difference is the swap's market value. (The method described elsewhere for determining the compensation due in a termination or sale—calculating the difference between the present values of the fixed cash payments remaining on the old swap and those of a current par swap with the same maturity and similar terms—is basically equivalent, since these two swaps' floating legs will be identical. The technique outlined here is more general, since it doesn't rely on the existence of a current matching par transaction.)

To calculate the PV of the fixed leg, the first step is to compute the fixed payment due on each of the remaining payment dates. This is done by multiplying the notional principal times the fixed rate and the appropriate day-count adjustment—the actual number of days in the payment period divided by the number of days in the year. Every payment is then discounted to its present value using the relevant zero-coupon rate. This rate represents the yield of a zero-coupon swap initiated now and maturing on the payment's delivery date; it is derived from the par swap curve, which graphs the coupons of at-market swaps with different maturities, as observed in the market. (Because zero-coupons' yields do not depend on the reinvestment of intermediary cash flows, they represent actual opportunity costs more accurately than par yields, which are weighted averages of these flows. For a discussion of the advantages of using the zero-coupon curve, and how it is derived, see "Interest Swap Valuation," by Benjamin Iben, in Beidleman, ed., listed in the *Bibliography*.) Finally, the PVs of all the payments are summed to get the PV of the fixed leg.

The procedure for valuing the floating leg is basically the same, with one wrinkle: Since no one knows exactly what the index level will be on any of the future payment dates, you have to use the rates implied by the market, as embodied in the forward yield curve, also derived from the par swap curve. (Note also that the day-count convention is different—actual/360.)

To see how the process works, consider an existing three-year swap, initiated on 10/12/93 and maturing 10/15/96, which pays a fixed coupon of 7.27 percent semiannually against six-month Libor on a $100 million notional principal. The chart on the next page illustrates the derivation of the two legs' PVs as of 10/12/94, one year into the swap's tenor (adapted from Finard).

The swap's market value is $13,446,548 – $12,859,808 = $586,740. To the fixed payer, this is a negative value; to the fixed receiver, it's positive. In other words, the swap currently is bankable only for the fixed receiver, which could receive $586,740 by selling (assigning) it on the market. On the other hand, this same sum also represents the receive-fixed counterparty's credit-risk exposure, since that is what it would have to pay someone to take over the pay-fixed leg on the original terms in case of a default (*see* **RISK**).

Prices for new par swaps can be derived using the inverse of this process, solving for the semiannual fixed bond rate that produces a cash stream with the same present value as that generated by the corresponding strip of floating rates. These future floating rates can't be derived from the par curve, however, since that is what's being solved for. Instead, they are deduced from a strip of six-month Eurodollar futures contracts covering the same period as the swap. These strip-implied rates are used to calculate the future floating payments, which are in turn used to generate an implied zero-coupon curve (graphing the zero-coupon rates that would produce the same terminal values). This curve provides the discount rates used, finally, to

FIXED LEG		
Payment Date	**Day-count Adj.**	**Rate**
4/12/95	182/365	7.27%
10/12/95	183/365	7.27%
4/12/96	183/366	7.27%
10/15/96	186/366	7.27%

FLOATING LEG		
4/12/95	182/360	5.94%
10/12/95	183/360	6.85%
4/12/96	183/360	7.13%
10/15/96	186/360	7.55%

derive the fixed bond-basis rate generating the same cash flow. (For a more detailed, and technical, discussion plus a sample derivation, see Marshall and Kapner, pages 146–53.)

This method is rarely used for swaps with tenors longer than five years, however. The cutoff reflects the fact that Eurodollar futures contracts with delivery dates farther out than five years are generally illiquid. This is important for two reasons. First, it means that the implied index levels used in the procedure are unavailable or not reliable for periods more than five years forward. Second, it limits the use of the contracts as alternatives to, and hedges for, swaps.

An interest-rate swap functions much like a strip of cash-settled futures contracts on deposits paying the swap-coupon rate: Each payment date corresponds to the expiration of a contract, when the difference between the coupon rate and the actual index level is paid out. Since such strips are easily constructed for periods up to five years, they present a viable alternative to end users considering short-term financial strategies involving interest-rate swaps. Similarly, a

Payment	0-coupon Rate	PV of Cash Flows
$3,625,040	6.00%	$3,519,914
$3,644,958	6.50%	$3,418,971
$3,635,000	6.74%	$3,289,675
$3,694,590	6.97%	$3,217,988
	Total =	$13,446,548

Payment	0-coupon Rate	PV of Cash Flows
$3,002,990	6.00%	$2,915,903
$3,482,080	6.50%	$3,266,191
$3,624,410	6.74%	$3,280,091
$3,900,830	6.97%	$3,397,623
	Total =	$12,859,808

dealer can use a Eurostrip to hedge a short-term swap for which it has not yet found a match. As a result, the two instruments are priced competitively, for maturities up to five years.

Beyond this point, however, strips can't be constructed, and the capital markets take over as sources of both swap competition and swap hedges. Consequently, the pricing method for long-term swaps is capital-markets arbitrage (*see the discussion of arbitrage in Chapter 2*).

The logic behind the arbitrage-pricing approach is that a swap dealer must make synthesizing debt at least as attractive as direct issuance. Say Buoy Co. is a BB-rated manufacturer that would like fixed-rate funding. For a synthetic approach to appeal, the cost to Buoy of borrowing at a floating rate and swapping into fixed must be no greater than that of issuing a fixed bond directly; on the other side, if AA-rated Anchor Corp. is to bite, selling a fixed bond and swapping to floating must cost it no more than simply borrowing at a floating rate in the first place (for formal expression of this insight, see box below).

The costs associated with the swap-plus-bond strategy must be no greater than those associated with direct issuance:

$$\text{Libor} + M_A + C_{Afl} \geq R_A + C_{Afix} - S + \text{Libor} + C_{As}$$
$$R_B + C_{Bfix} \geq \text{Libor} + M_B + C_{Bfl} - \text{Libor} + S + C_{Bs}$$

where:

S is the swap coupon

M_A and M_B are the margins (possibly negative) that Anchor and Buoy, respectively, must add to Libor when borrowing at a floating rate

R_A and R_B are the at-par coupons that Anchor and Buoy would have to pay on fixed-rate issues

C_{Afl} and C_{Bfl} are Anchor's and Buoy's costs for issuing floating-rate debt

C_{Afix} and C_{Bfix} are the two companies' costs for issuing fixed-rate debt

C_{As} and C_{Bs} are their costs for buying and administering the swap

The two equations can be combined and rearranged as

$$R_A + C_{Afix} - M_A - C_{Afl} + C_{As} \leq S \leq R_B + C_{Bfix} - M_B - C_{Bfl} - C_{Bs}$$

This indicates lower and upper bounds for the fixed swap coupon: The lower bound is the fixed-rate bond coupon minus the spread to Libor that higher-quality issuer Anchor would have to pay in the market, adjusted for its costs of issuance and maintenance; the upper bound is the fixed bond coupon minus the spread to Libor, adjusted for expenses, of lesser-quality Buoy.

The dealer sets its midrate somewhere within this range (for a long-dated swap) or (for a short-dated one) at the fixed rate arrived at by the process outlined earlier. It then subtracts from and adds to this rate the same number of basis points. The result is its bid-ask spread, representing the (lower) fixed rate it will be willing to pay and the (higher) one it be willing to receive in a swap.

The size of the spread reflects several factors. One of these is credit risk: The dealer may lower its bid or raise its ask rate to compensate for what it calculates as the probability that a counterparty will default. Another factor is supply and demand. For example, there may be more lower-rated issuers wanting to swap into fixed-rate debt than higher-quality ones willing to take the opposite side of the transaction. To balance its books, the dealer may raise its ask quote, thus discouraging pay-fixed counterparties, and also raise its bid, to make the receive-fixed side more attractive. A large volume of investors seeking to do asset-based swaps can also make spread adjustments necessary.

The swap dealer takes into account as well the availability of hedging instruments and their cost. Plain-vanilla interest-rate swaps are relatively easy to hedge. A dealer taking the pay-fixed side of a swap, for instance, might simultaneously buy a U.S. Treasury with the same maturity. This protects it against market risk from rate changes that could occur while it searches for a match: If rates fall, the swap will lose and the bond gain value; if rates rise, the opposite will happen. The dealer's hedging cost in this case is the difference between the Libor payments it receives from the swap and the interest it pays to finance its bond purchase. When the carry is negative—the interest rate is higher than Libor—the dealer may raise its ask to compensate; when positive, it might be willing to come down a few basis points.

Pricing most other types of swaps is done by reference to or through modification of these procedures. Currency swaps, for instance, can be priced by exploiting the interest-rate parity theorem.

The parity theorem holds that, because of arbitrage, the difference between interest rates in two different currencies should be reflected in their forward exchange rates, so that real returns across currencies are equalized. In other words, if a one-year instrument pays 7 percent in the U.S. and only 4 percent in Germany, then the one-year forward deutsche mark–dollar exchange rate must reflect an appreciation from the current one of approximately 3 percent, to offset the interest-rate difference; given a current exchange rate of 2 marks to the dollar, the one-year forward rate should be approximately 1.94 to 1. (*For a fuller discussion, see interest-rate parity in Appendix A.*)

A consequence of this theorem is that if you know the interest-rate swap coupons for two different currencies, you can derive the rates for swaps between these currencies. Say two-year deutsche mark interest-rate swaps are priced at 6.54 percent against six-month DM Libor and dollar swaps at 7.32 percent against six-month U.S.$ Libor. This implies the following two-year currency-swap rates (from Marshall and Kapner):

DM	6.54%	vs	US	7.32%
US	7.32%	vs	DM	Libor
DM	6.54%	vs	US	Libor
US	Libor	vs	DM	Libor

Pricing an off-market swap, as described above, basically involves bringing cash streams into balance. Amortizing and accreting swaps can usually be handled simply by varying the notional basis used in calculating future cash streams according to the schedule. Timing variations often involve increased credit risk or hedging costs, which are reflected in the dealer's spread.

NOTE: Different dealers may very well give you different quotes for the same structure. This reflects the fact that pricing is not strictly by the numbers. It depends on many factors, including liquidity of the market, the availability of hedges and how well these match the transaction, the ease with which offsetting swaps can be transacted, and the risk profile of the dealer's overall portfolio.

QUANTRO
(see NONGENERIC SWAPS)

REVERSAL

FOR SEVERAL REASONS, you might want to get out of a swap before it matures: you may no longer hold the underlying asset or liability it was designed to hedge; or the market may have turned against you and you want to cut your losses; or the opposite may have happened and you want to realize your profit. In these situations, you have three options: termination or assignment—both discussed elsewhere—or reversal.

In a reversal, you enter into a new swap that is more or less the mirror image of an existing one. For example, if you're paying 10.5 percent against six-month Libor on a plain-vanilla swap and the swap coupon rises to 11 percent, you might decide to enter into a new par swap as the receive-fixed counterparty. You thus realize your current profit on the old swap, spreading it out over the remaining tenor in the form of the 50bp difference between the two fixed rates (*see diagram*). In the opposite situation, where rates fall, you'd be spreading out a loss.

Reversal

In contrast, an assignment would return you that profit in one lump sum. This might be preferable if you want to recognize income in the current period. An assignment also relieves you of the credit risk from the original swap, while the reversal adds on another exposure, from the new swap. On the other hand, you don't need your original counterparty's approval to do a reversal, as you do in an assignment.

RISK

MOST DISCUSSIONS of the risks involved in swaps focus on dealers. They, after all, run bigger and more varied ones than most end users. Every swap a dealer does—a sizable number—exposes it to multiple risks: that the counterparty will default, that foreign-exchange or interest rates will move before it can arrange an offsetting transaction, that the offset it finally does arrange will be imperfect, not to mention the risk of termination because of legal or regulatory changes.

That said, end users have plenty to worry about. Many of a dealer's risks have counterparts for counterparties, perhaps smaller but nonetheless real. And dealers can use their large portfolios to net, disperse, and offset risk. Smaller users don't have the same resources. For them, the best protection is a good monitoring system, with policies for requiring credit enhancements, such as letters of credit or collateral, limiting exposure to a single counterparty, and handling market-value losses.

MARKET RISK A dealer is exposed to market risk because of the lag that usually occurs between arranging a swap and finding a counterparty to take the opposite side. Say that it arranges a five-year interest-rate swap for a pay-fixed client and rates proceed to rise. Like a bond, the receive-fixed leg of the swap loses value—the coupon is now below market, and the dealer will have to pay a higher rate on an offsetting swap. The dealer's bid-ask spread will insulate it from losses to some extent, but profits will nevertheless be squeezed. A similar situation could arise if the five-year rate remains unchanged during the lag period but the yield curve steepens around it (shorter terms fall and longer ones rise), since swap coupons are determined in part by expected future rates (*see* **PRICING**).

As an end user, you run market risk, too. If you're a pay-fixed counterparty and rates fall, so does your swap value. This is only a paper loss until you have to liquidate your position, but meanwhile you make larger and larger net payments (or get smaller and smaller ones) as the floating rate you receive decreases relative to the fixed rate you pay.

MISMATCH RISK For a dealer, mismatch risk arises from its inability to arrange offsetting swaps with the same notional principal as an existing one, or with the same payment and reset dates, the same maturity, or the same floating index. Any one of these discordances could prove costly. For example, if the dealer has to make a payment on one swap on June 10 but doesn't receive the offsetting payment from another until June 15, it is exposed to a default by the second counterparty, which would leave it holding the bag. In addition, if it has had to borrow to make the first payment, it incurs financing costs.

Since end users can customize swaps to their needs, you'd think they wouldn't have this type of problem. But they may actually create a mismatch to increase return. Say you're the treasurer of a BB-rated corporation that wants to use swap arbitrage to lower its fixed borrowing costs. You could do a fixed-for-Libor liability swap on an underlying floating-rate note also indexed to six-month Libor. But to really reduce costs, you opt instead to combine the swap with commercial paper that you roll over every 30 days. The CP rate is generally lower than equivalent Libor, because of the implicit call: When the paper matures, investors have the option of not renewing, or renewing on different terms. Moreover, if the yield curve is positive, 30-day rates will be lower than six-month ones. As a result, under normal circumstances, the Libor you receive from the swap will be higher than the CP rate you pay on your loan, and the difference can be subtracted from your fixed rate of borrowing.

Of course, every reward has a risk. In this case, it's posed by the mismatches you've introduced in reset and payment dates and interest-rate basis. If the curve inverts, for example, the 30-day rate you pay on the loan will climb above the six-month interest you earn on the swap. Even if the slope remains positive, a general rise will be reflected far sooner in your loan rate, which resets every 30 days, than in your semiannual Libor receipts. And if your credit rating deteriorates, CP investors may require that you pay a greater spread on your next rollover, but you'll continue to receive Libor flat. Any of these events would reduce or reverse your savings.

LEGAL RISK Several American banks learned the hard way about legal risk in the late 1980s, through their dealings with the London borough of Hammersmith & Fulham. The borough ran up huge losses on speculative interest-rate swaps it had arranged with the banks, then refused to pay up. Its auditor argued that the contracts governing the transactions were void, since they were "beyond the power of local authorities." The British courts agreed, and the Americans were effectively, and expensively, stiffed.

End users generally don't have to worry about the legal authority of their counterparties, which are usually swap dealers. They can, however, be affected by changes in law or regulations. For instance, if a government decides to impose a new withholding tax on swaps, the counterparty required to pay might decide to exercise the termination clause of the agreement.

CREDIT RISK Similarly, an end user—which generally gives its swap business to a few highly rated financial institutions—has fewer concerns about credit and default risk than dealers, which run large swap portfolios with multiple counterparties of various credit qualities. Nevertheless, the Group of 30 guidelines (*see* **MARKING TO MARKET** *and Chapter 3*) recommend that every swap participant track its credit as well as market exposures.

The term credit risk denotes the likelihood that your counterparty will fail to perform its obligations under the swap; default risk, the financial damage you'll sustain if it does fail. (In the literature, these terms are sometimes interchanged, or one or the other used for both aspects; the usage here was chosen as most logical.) The financial damage is your cost of replacing the swap, calculated as the present value of the difference between its remaining payments and those you'd get from a swap with the same maturity but the current, less favorable, terms (*see* **MARKING TO MARKET** *and* **PRICING***; also Chapter 3*).

Say you hold the receive-fixed leg of a $10 million 10 percent-for-Libor five-year swap that you entered into three years ago. The current two-year swap rate is 9.5 percent. If your counterparty were to default now, you'd be faced with a choice. You could enter into a two-year swap with a new pay-fixed counterparty at the prevailing terms, accepting the fact that your fixed receipts will be $25,000 lower from now on. Or you could retain the original, now-off-market, swap rate, compensating your new counterparty with an up-front payment of $89,166. This sum—the present value of four $25,000 payments to be made semiannually over the next two years, starting in six months—is your swap's replacement cost.

As this example illustrates, default risk is the inverse of market risk, a sort of black cloud around a silver lining: You're exposed only if the market has moved in your favor, making your side of the swap worth more than par. The good news is that you could sell it for a tidy sum in the market; the bad news is that you'd have to lay out the same sum to replace it if your counterparty reneged. (The example also illustrates another piece of good news: that your default exposure is always considerably less than the swap's principal.)

Credit/default risk, while bilateral, is asymmetrical—that is, though either counterparty could potentially suffer from a default by the other, only one is actually exposed on a particular date. Moreover, the overall risk of the swap is generally greater for one side than the other. This is a function not only of counterparty creditworthiness but also of term structure and swap design.

All other things being equal, fixed payers pose less risk to fixed receivers than vice versa. This is because rates have a floor—theoretically, zero; practically, somewhat higher—but no theoretical ceiling. So the fixed receiver's losses in a default are limited, and the payer's are not.

Moreover, when the yield curve is positive, the fixed payer's credit and default risks get larger with time. Swaps are designed so that the present values of the cash streams to both sides are equal. Consequently, when rates are expected to rise, the fixed leg is set higher than the current floating rate, under the assumption that this relationship will reverse as time goes by. There is very little chance that the fixed receiver will default early in the swap, when it is taking in the netted payments. The likelihood increases when the fixed payer becomes the one getting the swap income, finally balancing out its early outlays. A default at this point leaves it still on the short side and, moreover, looking for a replacement at a time when rates—including swap coupons—have risen (*see diagram*).

Finally, the risks are greater in a nonamortizing than

Cash-Flow Structure Assuming A Positively-Sloped Yield Curve

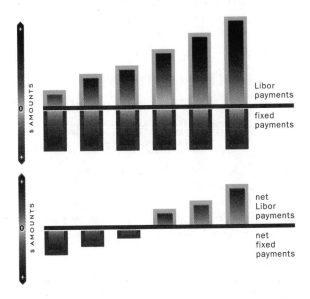

in an amortizing swap, and if the purpose is speculation rather than hedging. In an amortizing swap, the payments get smaller over time; this reduces both the likelihood that one counterparty won't be able to make them and the size of the cash stream forfeited if it can't. Similarly, if you construct a hedge properly, the circumstances in which you owe net payments under the swap should be the very ones that drive your business cash flows higher; exactly the opposite may be true in a speculative transaction.

NOTE: Futures exchanges have recently gotten into the act by offering services intended to reduce the costs and complications of handling credit exposure. The primary focus is on managing collateral, which has become increasingly popular among large OTC-derivatives players as a form of covering credit risk: in 1994, according to ISDA figures, approximately 10 percent of the net replacement value of new swaps was collateralized, compared with only 1 to 2 percent three years earlier. Although the exchanges' services are largely aimed at dealers, they might benefit end users as well, by taking some of the worry and back-office work out of marking to market and margining.

ROLLER-COASTER SWAPS
(see NONGENERIC SWAPS)

STRUCTURED NOTES AND TRANSACTIONS

COMBINE A SECURITY with one or more derivatives, then package the cash flows you've created as a bond that offers investors the market or product exposure they want and can't get elsewhere. That's pretty much the recipe for a structured note. Strictly speaking, instruments as simple as callable fixed-rate bonds fall under this definition. In practice, however, the term is reserved for more complex structures, often created or hedged with swaps.

One of the simplest is the securitized asset swap. This usually involves repackaging existing securities in a form more appealing to investors. For instance, in the mid-1980s Merrill Lynch discovered that investors were eager for fixed-rate dollar-denominated debt of the United Kingdom and were willing to accept 9.375 percent per annum for a three-year maturity. The closest instrument available in the market at the time was a $2.5 billion issue of seven-year notes, due October 1992 and paying three-month U.S.$ Libid (the London Interbank Bid Rate). So Merrill bought $100 million of these and did a swap with Prudential Global Funding Corp., exchanging three-month Libid for fixed payments equivalent to 9.375 per annum. It then arranged a three-year Eurobond issue with a 9.375 coupon funded by the swap payment, thus giving the public what it wanted.

The same technique has proved useful to underwriters seeking to unload unpopular securities. Morgan Guaranty, for instance, used currency swaps to repackage an issue of Kingdom of Denmark U.S. dollar–denominated notes that it had lead managed. The notes' coupon of 12.5 basis points under U.S.$ Libid had been overly optimistic. With the aid of floating-to-floating dollar-pound and dollar–deutsche mark currency swaps, however, Morgan transformed the issue into mark and pound FRNs, which found favor with many investors who had snubbed its original incarnation.

It's just a short logical step from this type of engineering to creating customized cash flows from scratch, using only derivatives like swaps and options. What results is sometimes termed a hybrid security or swap.

The creative process usually goes something like this: An investor expresses interest in an exotic form of debt; a banker finds a borrower willing to sell it (sometimes helping with pricing and marketing); then the borrower swaps the issue into its preferred form of funding, often with the banker as counterparty. The resulting instrument gives the investor a way to do something—make a bet, match a liability, access a market—that, for various reasons, would be impossible using the securities available in the market. Because the note is custom-tailored, the borrower gets a good price for it, which drives down its funding costs. The banker may get to offset another position in its swap book and, meanwhile, rakes in the fees.

To see how this works, consider a type of structured security that has had a fair amount of popularity, as well as notoriety: the leveraged inverse floating-rate note. The coupon on an inverse floater is determined by subtracting the level of a specified index from a fixed rate—for instance, 15 percent minus six-month Libor. The payment received rises as the index falls. To make the note more sensitive—that is, to boost the effect that each percentage-point change in rates will have on the payout—it is often leveraged. This is accomplished by multiplying the coupon formula times some constant. Modifying the formula given above to 30 percent minus 2 x Libor, for example, would double the sensitivity of the note. In addition, a minimum payment of zero, or a little above, is usually specified.

Issuers of structured notes typically hedge them with swaps that completely offset the coupon payments. Say Antipodes Corp. sells $100 million of a two-year inverse floater whose coupon is determined by the 30 percent minus 2 x Libor formula. To hedge this, it could arrange a two-year swap in which it received 30 percent minus 2 x Libor on a notional $100 million. In return, it would pay Libor minus a spread. The issuer also has to buy an interest-rate cap with a strike of 15 percent, to hedge the floor implicit in the minimum payment. The margin below Libor on the floating side of the swap thus has to be large enough—say, 10bp—to cover the cap purchase and still leave the issuer with attractive Libor funding.

The dealer acting as counterparty also has to hedge its exposures. It can do this with two swaps: In one, it would receive the at-market two-year fixed rate (say, 10.4 percent) in return for Libor, on a notional $200 million; in the other, the at-market rate minus 10bp in return for Libor minus 10bp, on $100 million (*see diagram*).

Other possible structures include indexed amortizing notes (IAN), index-differential notes (IDN), and synthetic convertible notes (SCN). The first two are securitized versions of the swaps described under **NON-GENERIC SWAPS**. The yield of an SCN, which typically pays a low coupon, comes mainly from the amount of principal returned at maturity. This amount is linked, through a redemption formula, to the performance of

Leveraged Inverse Floating-Rate Note

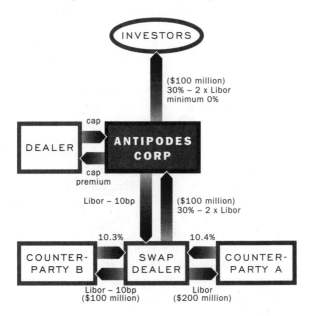

some benchmark, such as an interest, commodity, or equity index, or a specific stock or basket of stocks. For example, a five-year SCN might return to an investor a semiannual 2 percent coupon plus, at maturity, a sum determined by the formula:

$$\text{Par} + \text{Par} \times (\text{S\&P}_{maturity} - \text{S\&P}_{settle})/\text{S\&P}_{settle}$$
where the minimum return is par

In other words, the investor receives par times 100 percent plus the percent increase in the index. Again, the issuer hedges the payments by doing a swap (to receive the note coupon, plus a maturity payment of the excess redemption principal, in return for Libor minus a margin) and buying an option on the index.

The return of an index-differential note is linked to the spread between two interest rates—10-year and 30-year Treasury yields, for example. An IDN may have fixed coupons and variable principal, or variable coupons and fixed principal. It can involve two different currencies or different maturities within one currency. Usually, though, all payments are in dollars, allowing U.S.–based investors to express views on interest rates abroad without exposure to currency risk.

A two-year cross-currency, variable-coupon IDN might make semiannual payments, in dollars, equal to twice the difference between deutsche mark and dollar Libor, minus 4.95 percent. A purchaser of this note gains if the spread between the two Libors widens and loses if it narrows, regardless of the absolute level of either rate. The issuer's hedge involves a set of interest-rate swaps (paying fixed against DM Libor and receiving fixed for U.S.$ Libor) plus an option on the spread, since the coupon may never fall below zero.

As pointed out above, structured notes like these can be valuable investment or funding vehicles. A borrower can get cheaper debt by tailoring its notes to special requirements. An institutional investor can diversify its

portfolio by buying notes with returns linked to markets it can't enter directly. A hedger can match princi-
pal-redemption formulas to liability payouts, or create
cash flows that correlate negatively with those of existing assets. A speculator can customize return profiles
to suit a particular view on bond, equity, or commodity prices, or on the relationships between them.

A structured note simplifies accounting and tracking for the investor by uniting in a single security cash
flows from multiple transactions that would otherwise
have to be handled separately. That doesn't mean,
however, that the notes themselves are simple. In
fact, they require a fair degree of sophistication.

Getting a relatively high payout in return for a risk
that seems unlikely to materialize is not enough. You
have to be able to assess a note's fair market value. You
should also determine its performance in different scenarios and how well it fits with the risk profile of your
overall portfolio. To accomplish any of these tasks, you
may have to decompose it into the swaps, options, and
securities used to create or hedge it. For example,
many investors expect a yield-curve note, with a return
linked to the spread between two maturities, to trade
like a normal floater, but because of its composition it
actually behaves more like an intermediate-term bond:
It appreciates in value as the curve steepens, but loses
quickly as it flattens.

In other words, if you buy or issue structured notes,
you should understand financial engineering. A note's
price is related to the cost of hedging its cash flows.
This could also be a valuable guide if you have to liquidate a position you hold. Since these instruments are
tailored to particular requirements, they may have a
very small pool of potential buyers; if you can't tap one
for your note, you might have to unwind the various
transactions that went into its creation.

All this boils down to a familiar lesson: It's not the
note itself but ignorance of how it works that's dan-

gerous. Never put yourself in the position of relying solely on the salesman to tell you the price or performance characteristics of the instrument you're buying or issuing.

SWAPTIONS
(see NONGENERIC SWAPS)

SYNTHETIC CONVERTIBLE NOTES
(see STRUCTURED NOTES)

YIELD-CURVE SWAPS
(see NONGENERIC SWAPS)

ZERO-COUPON SWAPS
(see NONGENERIC SWAPS)

GLOSSARY

Arbitrage Exploiting the differences between the costs of similar items in different markets to make a risk-free profit. For example, an arbitrageur might buy a stock on the Boston exchange for $1 a share and simultaneously sell it in New York for the going price there of $1.05, locking in a profit of 5 cents a share.

Basis point One hundredth of a percent; for example, the difference between 6.0 percent and 6.01 percent.

Bid-ask spread = pay-receive spread The difference between the highest price a dealer will pay a seller of an item and the lowest price it will accept from a buyer of the same item. In referring to interest-rate swaps, the spread denotes the difference between the fixed rate the dealer will agree to pay and the fixed rate it will agree to receive.

Bond basis The day-count convention (see below) used to determine the interest payments of bonds, both government and corporate.

Bullet bond A bond that provides periodic fixed interest payments and repays principal in full at maturity, not before.

Call (see **Option**).

Carry The interest you earn from securities you hold minus the cost of the funds you borrowed to buy them; positive when the earned interest is greater, negative when the funding cost is greater.

Collateralized mortgage obligation (CMO) A mortgage-backed security (see below) that divides the underlying mortgage pool into different classes, called tranches, each of which pays a different interest rate and has a different maturity, usually two, five, ten, or 20 years.

Commercial paper A short-term unsecured debt instrument often used by banks and companies to obtain financing directly from investors, usually traded at a discount.

Constant-Maturity Treasury (CMT) An index tied to the yield of a synthetic security whose maturity remains the same from day to day; for example, the value of the five-year Constant-Maturity Treasury on any day is the yield of a Treasury whose maturity date is five years from that day. These yields are derived from the curve that the U.S. Treasury Department constructs daily using the closing market bid yields of actively traded Treasuries.

Counterparty One of the participants in a derivatives contract, such as a swap.

Credit spread = credit premium = quality spread The difference, usually quoted in basis points, between the interest rates paid by issuers of different credit quality on bonds having the same maturity; the recompense investors demand for taking on the credit risk of a lesser-quality issuer.

Day-count convention The numbers of days assumed

to be in a month and in a year when calculating the interest accrued on a debt instrument. Treasury notes and bonds employ the "actual over actual" convention, meaning that calculations use the actual number of days that have passed in the period, divided by 365 (or, in a leap year, 366) days in the year. U.S. corporate bonds use "30 over 360," assuming 30 days in a month and 360 days in a year; money-market instruments, including those paying Libor, use "actual over 360."

To calculate T-bond interest accrued on $10,000 from October 1 through December 1 at an annual rate of 10 percent, for instance, you would divide 61 (the number of days in October and November) by 365 and multiply this by 10,000. Then you'd multiply the result by 0.10:

$$61/365 \times 10,000 \times 0.10 = \$167.12$$

The formula for corporate interest at the same rate would be

$$60/360 \times 10,000 \times 0.10 = \$166.67$$

And for Libor

$$61/360 \times 10,000 \times 0.10 = \$169.44$$

Discount bond A bond selling below its face value.

Effective date = value date The date on which an agreement takes effect; in swaps, when interest begins to accrue.

Eurocurrency Currency on deposit outside its home country (not necessarily in a European bank); for example, U.S. dollars on deposit in a bank in Tokyo.

Exercise price = strike price The price at which the security underlying an option can be bought, in the case of a call, or sold, in a put (see **Option**).

Expiration date The date after which an option is void.

Floating-rate note (FRN) A debt security whose coupon is reset periodically to the current level of some index.

Forward contract An agreement to buy or sell a specified amount of a commodity, currency, or financial instrument at a price agreed on now, with delivery and settlement set for a future date.

Forward exchange rate The foreign-currency exchange rate for transactions that will occur at a specified date in the future.

Forward yield curve A curve of the expected future interest rates implied by current multiperiod rates; for example, the six-month forward 1-year rate is inferred from the current 1-year and 1.5-year rates.

Futures contract Like a forward contract (above) except it is traded on an exchange; after the trade is cleared, the exchange clearinghouse is the ultimate counterparty and requires margin deposits, typically adjusted to contract market value each day.

Guaranteed investment contract (GIC) A contract between an insurance company and an investor in which the company guarantees to pay a specified return on principal placed with it.

Interest-rate parity A relationship between the interest rates and spot and future currency-exchange rates for two countries' currencies implying that real interest rates for equivalent instruments in these two currencies will be the same. For example, if a one-year instrument pays 7 percent in the U.S. and only 4 percent in Germany, then the one-year forward deutsche mark–dollar exchange rate must reflect an appreciation from the current rate of approximately 3 percent; so given a current exchange rate of 2 marks to the dollar, the one-year forward rate should be approximately 1.94 to 1.

Parity results from arbitrage pressures. In the situation described above, German investors wishing to take advantage of the higher U.S. rate might borrow 200 marks at 4 percent and convert them to 100 dollars, to be invested at 7 percent and then reconverted at their investment's maturity, in a year. They would protect themselves against uncertain currency movements in the interim by agreeing to a one-year forward exchange rate—specifying the number of marks they will accept for their dollars in a year. If this number is higher than 1.94, they have locked in a profit. Seeing this, more investors would rush to do the same transactions, and their demand would drive the four rates (German and U.S. interest rates and both spot and forward deutsche mark–dollar exchange rates) into an equilibrium.

Internal rate of return (IRR) The discount rate that equates the present value of an investment's future cash flows with its initial cost.

Leverage A method of increasing an instrument's return by using borrowed funds or by multiplying the effect of a small change in some variable—for instance, tying a note's coupon to four times the appreciation in an index's return.

London Interbank Offered Rate (Libor) The rate international banks with the highest credit rating charge one another for large Eurocurrency loans (see above)—U.S.$ Libor for dollar loans, DM Libor for deutsche mark loans, £ Libor for pounds sterling loans, and so on; used as the basis for quoting most international floating rates.

Money-market basis The day-count convention (see above) used by money-market instruments; used in quoting Libor.

Money-market instruments Short-term debt instruments such as certificates of deposit, commercial paper, Treasury bills, repurchase agreements, and discount notes of government agencies; generally regarded as safe and highly liquid.

Mortgage-backed security A security whose payments to investors are tied to the interest and principal payments from an underlying pool of mortgages.

Nonbullet bond A bond that provides periodic fixed interest payments and may repay principal before maturity, for example through exercise of a call or put provision; a **call provision** gives the issuer the option of redeeming the bond early; a **put** gives investors the same option.

Over the counter (OTC) A dealer market in which transactions are conducted over a communications network rather than on the floor of an exchange; an instrument traded on such a market.

Option A contract that, in exchange for payment of a premium, confers the right, but not the obligation, to buy **(call)** or sell **(put)** a stated amount of a particular product at a specified price **(the strike)** within a specified time **(American-style)**, or on a specified date **(European-style)**.

Par bond A bond selling at its face value.

Par yield curve A curve graphing the yields, at various maturities, of an instrument valued at par.

Par swap curve A yield curve graphing the coupons for at-market swaps of various maturities.

Plain-vanilla swap The basic, or generic, form of an interest-rate, currency, commodity, or equity swap.

Premium (see **Option**).

Premium bond A bond selling above its face or redemption value.

Present value The value today of a sum or cash stream to be delivered in the future; derived by discounting the future sum by the appropriate interest rate or rates. The discount rates represent cost of opportunity—the future sum's value is reduced by the amount of interest you could have earned if you held it and invested it today. Zero-coupon yields (see below) are often used as discount rates because they don't involve intermediate cash flows and so entail no assumptions about future reinvestment rates; par bond yields, in contrast, which are also sometimes used, assume reinvestment of intermediate flows at the yield rate, and thus imply a flat yield curve.

Put (see **Option**).

Repurchase agreement Essentially a loan collateralized with government securities that the lender controls: the borrower sells government securities to the lender, agreeing to buy them back on a specified future date at a specified price that gives the lender a low-risk return, representing the "repo rate."

Reinvestment risk The risk that interim cash flows from an investment will have to be reinvested at interest rates different from those prevailing when the investment was acquired.

Semiannual rate (sa) An annual rate of interest that is compounded semiannually.

Spot exchange rate The foreign-currency exchange rate applicable for transactions occurring immediately (by convention, in two days).

Spot market The market for immediate delivery of a currency or commodity (that is, within two days), settled in cash.

Spot price The current market price for a commodity or stock.

Stress testing Measuring how large a change in price or risk will be produced in an instrument or portfolio by changes in financial variables such as interest and currency-exchange rates, yield-curve shape, and market volatility; also how the results of your tests would be affected if you changed your evaluation model, the way you constructed yield curves, or your assumptions about correlations among factors such as at-the-money and out-of-the-money volatility.

Tenor = maturity The period between a transaction's effective and termination dates.

Term structure The pattern of yields on debt instruments of the same quality but with different maturities, often graphed as a yield curve (see **yield curve**).

Termination date = maturity date The day a transaction terminates.

Yield curve A graph showing the level of interest rates as a function of time. The normal curve is positively sloped, or convex, with long-term rates higher than short-term ones; a negatively-sloped curve is concave, long-term rates having fallen below short-term ones.

Zero-coupon bond A deeply discounted bond that pays no interest until maturity, when it is redeemed at its full face value—the difference between this and its purchase price is its total return; it is thus free of re-investment risk (see above).

Zero-coupon yield curve A curve graphing the yields of a zero-coupon instrument at different maturities, derived from the par yield curve for the same instrument; often used to discount multiperiod cash streams to their present values (see above).

JOURNALS & ASSOCIATIONS

Journals

Derivatives Strategy A newsletter relaunched in November 1995 as a monthly magazine, covering derivatives, mostly from the perspective of U.S. end users, with style and (wonder of wonder) humor. Annual subscription: $245. 153 Waverly Place, Suite 1200, New York, NY 10014.

Derivatives Week A weekly newsletter, published by *Institutional Investor,* with short articles covering derivative-related news around the world. Annual subscription: $1,495. 488 Madison Ave, 14th Floor, New York, NY 10022.

Risk A glossy monthly magazine with a global perspective, covering all aspects of risk management, from short reports on related news and news makers to articles on developments in derivatives regulation, profiles, and treatises on measurement models. Annual subscription: $399. Subscription Department, *Risk* Publications, 104-112 Marylebone Lane, London W1M 5FU, UK.

Swaps Monitor A newsletter, appearing twice a month, directed to the financial risk–management professional; publishes swap-industry rates, spreads, and revenues, as well as short, trenchant articles on developments in accounting, legislation, and litigation, plus the personalities and firms involved in the market. Annual subscription: $1,000. Suite 705, 648 Broadway, New York, NY 10012.

Associations

International Swaps and Derivatives Association (ISDA) A New York–based trade organization of participants in the OTC derivatives market, including dealers, consultants, accounting and law firms, and corporate, governmental, and investment-management end users. Its functions include standardizing documentation, representing the industry position on regulatory and legislative issues, resolving market-practice disputes, publishing market surveys, and conducting educational seminars and conferences. Located at 1270 Avenue of the Americas, New York, NY 10020. For information, call Steven Kennedy at 1-212-332-1200.

British Bankers Association A London-based association that, like ISDA, promulgated a swaps code, the British Bankers Association Interest Rate Swap (BBAIRS) Terms. This was intended to help in documenting interbank swaps, and is now mainly used in Britain.

The End Users of Derivatives Association (Euda) A Washington, D.C.–based organization formed in 1994 to promote the interests of nondealers that engage in derivatives transactions. Members include corporations, government agencies, financial institutions, and nonprofit entities. Euda sends out monthly "Updates," which chronicle, from an end user's viewpoint, legal, tax, and accounting developments affecting derivatives, and publishes the quarterly newsletter *Derivatives Developments.* Located at 1275 Pennsylvania Avenue, NW, Suite 800, Washington, DC 20004-2404. For information call 1-202-383-0639 or e-mail EUDA@aol.com.

MARKET MAKERS

THE FOLLOWING LIST is excerpted from *Risk* magazine's September 1995 rankings, which were based on a poll of some 250 banks, brokers, and other derivatives dealers. Respondents were asked to name, in order, the three best banks in several product and currency categories, using criteria such as tight pricing, market-making reliability and liquidity, and innovation and speed of transaction. Of course, these are professionals' judgments, and their concerns might be different from yours. Still the list should give you an idea of the biggest and most active market participants.

Interest-Rate Swaps

US $

Chemical Bank
JP Morgan
Barclays/BZW

Swiss Bank Corp.
Fuji Capital Markets

DM

JP Morgan
Swiss Bank Corp.
Chemical Bank

£

NatWest Markets
Chemical Bank
HSBC Midland

¥

Chemical Bank
Fuji Capital Markets
Mitsubishi Finance

FFR

Société Générale
Banque Paribas
Banque Nationale de Paris

ECU

JP Morgan
Banque Paribas
São Paolo Bank

Currency Swaps

US$/DM

Deutsche Bank
JP Morgan
Bankers Trust

DM/¥

Dresdner Bank
Bank of Tokyo

CSFB
Merrill Lynch
Mitsubishi Finance

US $ / ¥

Bankers Trust
Sumitomo Bank Cap Markets
Industrial Bank of Japan

US $ / £

Barclays/BZW
NatWest Markets
HSBC Midland

DM / £

Barclays/BZW
HSBC Midland
NatWest Markets

US $ / FFR

Société Générale
Crédit Agricole
Banque Paribas

Equity-Index Swaps

S & P 500

Goldman Sachs
Union Bank of Switzerland
Morgan Stanley

DAX

Swiss Bank Corp.
Morgan Stanley
JP Morgan

NIKKEI 225

Nomura International

Société Générale
Bankers Trust
Goldman Sachs
JP Morgan

Swaptions

U S $

JP Morgan
Swiss Bank Corp.
Chemical Bank

D M

JP Morgan
Swiss Bank Corp.
Deutsche Bank

Y

JP Morgan
Banque Nationale de Paris
Chemical Bank

Indexed Amortizing Swaps

Merrill Lynch
Goldman Sachs
CSFB

BIBLIOGRAPHY

Anonymous. "Confessions of a Structured Note Sales-man." *Derivatives Strategy,* November 1995. Frightening insider's view of the structured-note market and insight into how it can exploit investors' biases and blindnesses.

Beidleman, Carl R., ed. *Interest Rate Swaps.* Homewood, Ill.: Business One, 1991. A collection of essays on interest-rate swaps, from general descriptions to more technical issues, written by contributors with experience in academia and financial transactions.

_____. *Cross-Currency Swaps.* Homewood, Ill.: Business One, 1992. A collection of essays, similar to those in *Interest Rate Swaps* (see above) but focusing on currency swaps.

Das, Satyajit. *Swap and Derivative Financing: The Global Reference to Products, Pricing, Applications and Markets,* revised ed. Chicago: Probus Publishing Co., 1994. Massive, and fairly dense, discussion of swaps and related derivatives.

Dattatreya, Ravi E. and Kensuke Hotta, eds. *Advanced Interest Rate and Currency Swaps.* Chicago: Irwin Professional Publishing, 1994. Essays on more advanced swap structures and swap applications, representing the points of view of academics, dealers, and end users.

Davis, Henry. "Brought to Account." *Risk,* October 1995. An article on new and possible future developments in accounting for swaps.

Derivatives—Current Accounting and Auditing Literature. A Report Prepared by the Financial Instruments Task Force of the Accounting Standards Executive Committee. New York: American Institute of Certified Public Accountants, 1994. A booklet on the current guidelines for auditing and accounting for derivatives.

Finard, Joel B. "A Blueprint for Valuing Interest-Rate Swaps." *Bank Accounting and Finance,* Winter 1994-5. An article outlining an approach to valuing swaps and describing some of the underlying principles.

Gastineau, Gary L. *Dictionary of Financial Risk Management.* Chicago: Probus Publishing Co., 1992. A dictionary with concise and clear entries for terms used in risk management both in the U.S. and Europe.

Marshall, John F. and Kenneth R. Kapner. *Understanding Swaps.* New York: John Wiley & Sons, 1993. A basic and clearly written introduction to the structures, their use, pricing, and risk management.

Marshall, John F., V.K. Bansal, A.F. Herbst, and A.L. Tucker. "Hedging Business Cycle Risk With Macro Swaps and Options." *Journal of Applied Corporate Finance 4* (1992).

_____. "Macro Swaps and Macro Options: the Next Frontier?" In *The Swaps Handbook: 1991-92 Supplement,* K.R. Kapner and J.F. Marshall, eds. New York: New York Institute of Finance, 1992.

The Principles and Practices for Wholesale Financial Market Transactions. A set of derivatives-trading guidelines prepared by the Federal Reserve Bank of New York together with ISDA, the Foreign Exchange Committee, the Emerging Markets Traders Association, the New York Clearing House Association, the Public Securities Association, and the Securities Industry Association.

Ruyter, Tina. "Don't Sign That Swap Contract...until you read this article." *Derivatives Strategy,* November 1995. Good tips on modifying an ISDA master agreement to suit your needs.

Schwartz, Robert J. and Clifford W. Smith, Jr. *The Handbook of Currency and Interest Rate Risk.* New York: New York Institute of Finance, 1990. A collection of essays on the evolution, theory, and application of risk-management tools, with global examples, by experts with hands-on experience.

Stewart, Jules. "Sterling Performance." *Risk,* August 1995. How Reuters uses swaps, as described by its deputy financial director.

Willis, Gerri. "Swapping for Dollars." *SmartMoney,* July 1995. How executives use equity swaps to diversify their compensation.

INDEX

About Bloomberg

THIS BOOK DRAWS on the extensive financial-information resources of **Bloomberg Financial Markets**. Bloomberg is a global, multimedia-based distributor of information services, combining news, data, and analysis for financial markets and businesses. Bloomberg provides real-time pricing, data, history, analytics, and electronic communications 24 hours a day, accessed currently by 180,000 financial professionals in 82 countries.

Bloomberg covers all key global securities markets, including Equities, Money Markets, Currencies, Municipals, Corporate/Euro/Sovereign Bonds, Commodities, Mortgage-Backed Securities, Derivative Products, and Governments. Bloomberg also delivers access to Bloomberg Business News, whose more than 350 reporters and editors in 67 bureaus worldwide provide around-the-clock coverage of economic, financial, and political events.

To learn more about Bloomberg—one of the world's fastest-growing real-time financial information networks—call a sales representative at:

Frankfurt:	49-69-920-410
Hong Kong:	852-2521-3000
London:	44-171-330-7500
New York:	1-212-318-2000
Princeton:	1-609-279-3000
Singapore:	65-226-3000
Sydney:	61-2-777-8600
Tokyo:	81-3-3201-8900

About the Author

Elizabeth Ungar, Ph.D., has taught at Trinity College, Dublin, and is a senior editor of both *Bloomberg Personal* magazine and *Bloomberg Magazine*, wherein she regularly converts highly technical subjects into highly readable prose. She has worked for *Business Month*; *Manhattan,inc.*; *Institutional Investor*; and *American Banker*. She also edited the book *An Introduction to Option-Adjusted Spread Analysis*, by Tom Windas, published by Bloomberg Press.